Break Your Wealth Ceiling

How ordinary people can create extraordinary wealth with real estate

Christian Dy

Published by Kimody Publishing, January 2024
ISBN: 9781738246502

Editor: Trevor McMonagle-The Right Words Editing
Typeset: Greg Salisbury-Red Tuque Books
Book Cover Design: Greg Salisbury-Red Tuque Books

Contents

Appendix

Introduction

"Two roads diverged in a wood, and I—
I took the one less traveled by,
And that has made all the difference."
Robert Frost

I have always believed that the quality of your life comes down to the quality of the questions you ask yourself. How satisfied are you right now with your wealth? Since you are reading this book, you likely want more out of life. If you are single, you dream of building wealth and enjoying life. If married, you love your kids, want financial security, and you want more for them. If you immigrated to this country, you have made all the sacrifices that immigrants tend to. Now you are hoping to give your children a better future. Maybe you were born in this country, and you have created wealth. Now you're afraid the next generation might squander it.

I've written this book as a gift that holds a message of wealth. I want to make every North American aware of a strategy that has been available for thousands of years, and has allowed generations of average citizens to create wealth beyond their income. Whether you decide to believe it, apply it, or share it will be up to you.

This book might be controversial; it might go against what you have already spent a few decades doing to build wealth. It will likely go against the philosophies of many people. And, in the end, it just might not agree with you, which is OK.

I am not writing about starting a business or a side hustle to create wealth, like many millionaires and billionaires have done. This book is for ordinary people with ordinary jobs, wanting a better investment strategy than what is being popularized. Traditional investing consists of investments such as mutual funds, index funds, or exchange-traded funds (ETFs). If you are a Do-It-Yourself (DIY) investor, you might also be investing in individual stocks. Most people are encouraged to use a dollar cost averaging strategy, which consists of investing an equal amount on a monthly basis. The strategy is popular because you do not have to try to time the market. If you use an advisor, they will charge you a management expense ratio (MER) to pick and manage the investments.

In this book, I will highlight the problems with traditional investing and explain an alternative strategy that will lead the average investor to significantly more wealth.

This strategy I have named the Dyhard Investment Portfolio (DIP), which is a variation on a portfolio that has been around for over a thousand years, hence the name Dyhard. For those Bruce Willis fans, it is a combination of the phrase "diehard" and my last name, "Dy." The DIP strategy is the approach taken at Latitude West Financial, the financial planning and investment practice that I established when I began my second career in the early 2000s. The DIP strategy will make sense to some readers because you might already be doing a version of it. But for traditional investors in the stock market, I will show you a better, alternative path to generate more wealth than you have previously imagined possible for yourself and your family.

This method is meant to break the generational cycle of financial mediocrity. In my financial journey, I've had many questions that I just could not understand.

- Why are well-educated people still struggling financially?
- What are self-made millionaires doing differently than everyone else?
- Is it possible to get double-digit returns on investments consistently in the long term?
- If dollar cost averaging index funds are such a good idea along the road to wealth, why aren't the ultrawealthy doing this?
- And finally, why are financial advisors not modeling what the best investors in the world are doing?

My story is the story of the Canadian immigrant, a common story that resonates with more people in Canada every year. It is a story of wanting more for our kids. It is a story of breaking a cycle of struggle. It is a story of ordinary people creating extraordinary wealth.

Let me define what I mean by "ordinary people." I am referring to Canadians who make between $50K and $150K of annual income as individuals, or households that make $100K to $300K. This will capture the majority of the middle class. When I refer to creating generational wealth, I mean having the ability to set up your kids and your grandkids with all educational expenses and down payments on a home or giving them a fully paid-for home.

This definition also means NOT taking from any of the wealth that you and your spouse need to live an abundant lifestyle, secure your future retirement, and allow for generous charitable endeavours. Because you have sacrificed enough, you too deserve to live an abundant life.

Currently, many people are following a set prescription for building wealth. It starts with getting an education and a good job. You then work hard and invest your money. You do all the right things with saving 10% of your income, maximizing your RRSPs each year, contributing to your kids' RESPs, taking two modest vacations per year, and being able to donate weekly to a faith organization. At retirement, you will be on a fixed budget to ensure you do not run out of money.

Following this financial path, will you still be able to have a comfortable retirement? Yes. Will you be rich? Unfortunately, no. This is a recipe for keeping people inside a mediocre wealth bracket. You will be mindful of not spending too much on purchases every week, and will likely worry about running out of money at the end of the month, year, and lifetime. Does this resonate with you? As well, you will likely raise your kids in a similar way, teaching them to follow your financial path. The good news is that there is a better path to becoming wealthy. You just need to take a slight detour in your journey. I believe we should all strive to become a wealthier version of ourselves. This book is a road map to that better path. It seeks to achieve three goals:

1. The option to retire early;
2. The option to set up two generations with wealth; and
3. The option to live significantly beyond your income.

Consider the story of Adam and Bob. They are the same age, have the same career, the same number of kids, and live in the same city. Bob was encouraged by his financial advisor to contribute to his TFSAs and RRSPs. He had a contribution-matching RRSP through work as well, and used RESPs to fund his kids' education. When his kids entered college, he had enough to support each of their tuitions. When he retired, Bob lived on a modest fixed income and enjoyed a lifestyle similar to what he had during his working years. When Bob passed away, he had depleted the majority of his retirement savings, and the remainder went to his children and wife.

Now, let us look at Adam. He was taught by his parents to invest money in real estate that created both capital appreciation and cash flow. His parents showed him how to use his TFSAs for a down payment on rental property. As his equity grew, he bought another property, and another, and continued to do this for over thirty years. When his children were in their twenties, he not only had paid for their education, but had also set each of them up with a down payment on their homes. Adam and his wife had enough monthly cash flow to take any annual vacation they wanted. Their rental cash flow and the equity in their properties allowed them to retire early. In retirement, they went on yearly trips, paying for both their kids and grandkids. They invested in recreation properties that created memorable moments for their family, and generated cash flow when they were not using them. In retirement, they are not worried about running out of money, but in lowering their taxation when passing millions of dollars in assets to the next two generations. They also changed lives through charitable donations, which included their local community, projects abroad, their church, as well as helping struggling family members.

Which of these two stories models your current financial future? Which story most resonates with your vision of an abundant life? Will maxing out your RRSPs, RESPs, and TFSAs take you there?

I have suggested what this book will do, but I also want to say what it will *not* do. This book is not about how to budget your money, nor how to get out of debt, nor how to invest in the stock market. If you are looking for how to get out of debt, then you might want to read Dave Ramsey's book *Total Money Makeover*. If you are looking for tips on picking stocks, try *One Up on Wall Street* by Peter Lynch. And if you want to DIY in real estate, Gary Eldridge's *Investing in Real Estate* or Don Campbell's *Real Estate Investing in Canada* are great reads.

What will my book do? It will debunk the idea that dollar cost averaging a balanced stock portfolio will make you wealthy and will explain how average Canadians can create a net worth beyond their imagination. Finally, it will show you what you need to do if you want to achieve greater wealth for yourself and set up your next two generations. In this book, I will share stories of my family members, my work colleagues, and my clients who are living a life of wealth, abundance, and generosity. All people should seek to grow in their journey of life. But realize, your comfort zone is not your growth zone. If you want greater wealth than you are experiencing now, then you need to be willing to do something that might not feel comfortable at the beginning such as using a fee-for-service advisor, or investing in real estate. If you keep an open mind, I assure you that by the end of this book you will have grown to a better understanding of how breaking your wealth ceiling is easier than you ever imagined.

Chapter 1: My Financial Beginning

"Life is difficult. Once we truly know that life is difficult-once we truly understand and accept it-then life is no longer difficult."
M. Scott Peck

Who is the greatest person you know? I've asked this question several times to audiences I was speaking in front of. Followed by, what criteria are you using to define greatness when choosing this person? Wealth, IQ, status, generosity, sacrifice? When I first read the book *Rich Dad, Poor Dad* by Robert Kiyosaki, I was shocked by the parallels between the writer's and my personal financial journeys. I was born in the Philippines and came to Canada at the age of two with my brother and my parents who wanted a better life for themselves and for their children. My aunt, our family's pioneer and so the first to arrive in Canada and go through the exciting process of immigrating, sponsored us. Once she was established here, she did what many immigrants do—they sponsor family members to come over as well.

My aunt, uncle, mother (Circa 1970)

Now consider this: In the early '70s, my mother and her siblings all immigrated to Canada around the same time. I had an uncle who was an engineer and my mother and aunt were both accountants. All three had the same parents, a similar educational background, and similar annual income. They were subject to the same challenges of finding work, struggling to save, raising kids, and of keeping a home in the '80s with the ultra-high interest rates.

My aunt, uncle, mother (Present day)

Now let's fast forward five decades. All of them are in their seventies, two of them still working part-time, even though past retirement age, in order to manage household expenses. They both owned their homes and had some modest savings. However, the third sibling, my uncle, was able to retire early, generated over $10K per month in net cash flow and owned over fifteen properties. Having retired early, he travels multiple times per year with his wife, drives new cars, has long vacations with friends and family, still pokes around for new investments, and essentially does whatever he wants to do. His years of sacrifice have long ended. Further, he was able to set up two generations of wealth in the form of down payments and education, thereby creating a head start for his descendants. This head start allowed them to pursue careers of passion, not necessity. The same wealth allowed him to be the go-to person for helping with life's financial surprises such as leaky roofs, wedding celebrations, and family trips.

This is the dream for many Canadians, to live a life of abundance, financial security, and generosity.

So, what was the difference between my uncle and his sisters? What was the secret of his wealth? My uncle prioritized investing in real estate to build his wealth in Canada. Once I discovered this, many more questions arose. Why weren't more people doing this? Where did he learn to do this? Why was this not being taught to other Canadians? I know that in Canada and the US, there is more than enough wealth and opportunity for the average person, so why is the information needed to grow wealth missing?

When I first started earning money, I did what many people do, invest in the stock market. This can come in the form of a balanced portfolio, an index fund, or some carefully chosen stocks. In Canada, you are likely investing through your TFSAs or RRSPs. If so, congratulations, this is the correct first step in building wealth. Getting started and sticking to a plan puts you ahead of most people. As well, if you are happy with your results and feel you are going to achieve all of your exciting goals, then you might not want to change anything that you are currently doing. You have done nothing wrong and should stick to your strategy. However, if your results have been disappointing, or you want to know how they can be improved, then please keep reading.

Whether you have been investing for one year or thirty years, now might be the time to re-examine if your current wealth plan will take you to a level of mere comfort or a level of outstanding abundance. Currently, my mother and aunt live a life of comfort, while my uncle lives a life of abundance. In my twenties, I wanted to shift my focus to wanting more from my investments. But, understanding how that was possible was my new challenge. With these questions, my journey began. I set out to find better financial information, live a life of abundance, and break my own wealth ceiling.

Chapter 2: Your Wealth Ceiling

"If you want to have more, you have to become more." Jim Rohn

All Canadians have a wealth ceiling. My definition of "wealth ceiling" is the amount of wealth you can expect to achieve in your lifetime, based on your income and your savings/investment habits.

Assume you are a doctor making $300K per year, living off 60% of your gross income, paying 30% taxes, and keeping 10% for investing. You start investing during your working years, which, after residency and paying down loans, is approximately thirty-five years of investing. If you retire at age sixty-five, with a 7% annual rate of return, your wealth ceiling would be $4,147,106, not including the value of your home.

For a teacher, with forty investable years, putting 10% of income toward retirement, plus pension, your wealth ceiling might be closer to $1.5M.

You might be reading this as a teacher or doctor nearing retirement, thinking you have nowhere close to this number. Conversely, you might have much more than these numbers. This is because we will all fall somewhere on a normally distributed graph. Note that I am not including those people who have a side job nor those who run a side business. I only want to include people who rely on their core income and their passive investments for wealth.

If you are spending more than four hours per week on

your investments, engaging in activities such as day trading or managing multiple rental properties, then I would also disqualify you from these calculations, considering these as active side hustles. If you have a type of automated investment system that takes less than a few hours per month to manage, including your stock investments or your multiple rental properties, then you would be included.

If you are the average person who invests 5% to 15% of your income using a traditional financial strategy—dollar cost averaging in a balanced portfolio—then in retirement, you can expect to stay at the same lifestyle level that your working years provided. This will entail taking similar vacations, dining at similar restaurants, and living in similar housing. The balanced portfolio strategy is designed to ensure you can maintain your current lifestyle expenses in retirement, without running out of money. This formula will keep you in a life of maintenance but will not create enough to break into a life of abundance or charity. It will simply be a life under your wealth ceiling.

Sensitivity Analysis

A sensitivity analysis is a way to measure how much an outcome swings up or down with minor adjustments to an input.

Let's take an average investor, aged twenty-five, who starts investing a modest monthly amount toward their retirement—$500 a month. This person continues that until age sixty-five, a total of forty years. At a 4% annual rate of return, they would have achieved a $580,531 . We can use this return as our base case. Below, we apply a sensitivity analysis to see how much the wealth grows if the rate of return is increased to 8%, then 12%.

	Total investment	Age 65 Total	Difference
4%	$240,000	$580,531	Base Case
8%	$240,000	$1,610,539	+177%
12%	$240,000	$4,850,510	+736%

When we change the number slightly to an 8% return, they would have achieved $1,610,539. At a 12% return, they would have achieved $4,850,510.

Notice how a 4% return increase can dramatically change the output. So, why do I use these numbers?

A 4% would be a very conservative return over a lifetime. An 8% return would be an S&P 500 average, even if you were to do it yourself. But a 12% return is a much higher return, and trying to achieve this in the stock market consistently would be considered almost impossible. So, for the average investor, the 12% return through the equity market is not likely.

For those DIY investors who are able to get double-digit returns, do not think they are now stock market experts. DIY investors always think they are geniuses when they get high returns, which is the case when the markets are up. But when they experience down markets, it is not so easy anymore. Professionals, though, are able to get consistent returns, regardless of what the markets are doing.

Traditionally, if a stock market investor wants higher returns, they need to expose themselves to higher volatility. At the time of this writing, Bitcoin is down 36% from its peak, and Tesla is down 34%. If these types of high-flying investments were delivering double-digit returns in your portfolio, you should ask: Is it possible to achieve double-digit returns more consistently? Is it possible to secure double-digits while reducing the volatility and not giving up on the returns?

Three Wise Men

In my first career as a high school calculus teacher, I was paid the same amount, regardless of ability and performance, as other teachers. Salary increments were based on years of service and level of university education. Minor salary adjustments did apply. Having a Master's degree, teaching in a particular school district, or working in a private rather than a public school would have some effect on salary. In general, however, all teachers make about the same income, unlike other professions such as tradesmen, contractors, dentists, and realtors, where the income differential can be significant.

During my time teaching, I came across three colleagues who were all wealthy beyond their income. I encourage you to read *The Millionaire Next Door* by Thomas Stanley. It describes what the average millionaire in the US actually looks like and debunks the myths of what they did to get there. If I focused on the stories of my three colleagues, this book would be called *The Millionaire Teacher in the Next Classroom.*

None of the three teachers had a side job, nor were they given any significant amount of wealth from their parents. All were able to take early retirement, and they all created wealth beyond a teacher's wealth ceiling. None of them solely relied on their pension, RRSPs, or TFSAs as their main source of wealth. They all had money in the stock market, but it was a minor portion of their assets. Their other asset class generated cash flow at four times their teacher's pension. As well, their net assets were in the millions prior to their departure from teaching. The average retiree household in Canada has $543K of net worth.

Average Net Worth

These three wise men each had roughly ten times this net worth prior to age sixty-five. If you were in an occupation where everyone made the same income, yet you had colleagues who would end up with ten times your net worth, wouldn't you want to know how?

There is only one answer: investment real estate.

Does this type of investment take a little extra work? Yes. Is it rocket science? No. Is it a get-rich-quick scheme? No. Day trading, shorting stocks, and investing in Bitcoin and other financial endeavours are also activities that I have known colleagues to engage in. However, none of them ever became wealthy in doing so. None were able to retire early with these investments. Most of them actually lost money.

What does a life of abundance look like for these three wise men? All three have recreational properties, on top of their other cash-flowing real estate properties. One has a five-bedroom house in Whistler, the other a house on the water in the Okanagan, and the other a property on the beach in Maui. Each property has the ability to be rented out for cash flow when they are not using it for personal enjoyment. These are teachers without a side hustle. They do not spend hours on their investments each week. They never made more than $80K annually at the peak of their teaching careers, and all retired early.

They have fit my description perfectly of living a rich life. They had the ability to fund their children's educational needs for two generations, as well as provide down payments for their housing. They retired early, enjoyed an abundant life of travel and helping their community. These three wise colleagues of mine have been wonderful role models for me, and I am grateful to them for inspiring me to break my own wealth ceiling.

Chapter 3: The DIP Strategy Explained

What exactly is the Dyhard Investment Portfolio strategy?

This is a method of investing that maximizes your money at different phases of your life. At each phase, an analysis is conducted to determine the best usage of your money depending on the available opportunities, your comfort level, and a cost-benefit analysis.

The DIP strategy can be summarized in three phases of growth.

Phase 1: Starting from Zero

When you have no money, such as at the beginning of your career, you need to start building wealth. If you just finished school, you might have student loans to pay back so the available opportunities are to pay back your loans (ex. 6%/a rate) or to invest the money, for example, in stocks or mutual funds.

Your comfort level is your first limitation. Not increasing comfort levels in investing is what keeps most people under their wealth ceiling and no one is comfortable with what they do not fully understand. You might be more comfortable with paying down your loans versus investing in the stock market if you have never invested in the stock market. However, these days, more young people are investing in the stock market on their own with online platforms such as Questrade. Their level of comfort is quite high due to the ease of the transactions, the numerous DIY online resources, and their peer groups investing.

Some people have a high comfort level with investing in individual stocks such as Tesla, Apple, or GameStop. Some will venture into high-flying assets such as Bitcoin and other cryptocurrencies. Unfortunately, many are experiencing the dramatic volatility when these assets move either up or down. Much like the feeling from a win in gambling, there is a financial high when your marijuana stock doubles after three months. Conversely, you are devastated when your Bitcoin investment is down 60% in one month. This type of investing can really turn you on to individual stock investing, or turn you off investing all together.

Unfortunately, the majority of people shy away from the asset class of real estate because they believe they are not at the right stage of life to be investing in properties. This is completely wrong thinking if you are trying to grow beyond your wealth ceiling. The majority of average Canadians I know who have assets in the hundreds of thousands in their twenties and in the millions in their thirties have accomplished this through real estate investing. And, they all started as early as possible.

A cost-benefit analysis is the necessary key to the DIP strategy. This is where the options you have to invest in are analyzed to determine which is the better option for you. To better understand, think of a road trip you are taking from Seattle to New York. People tend to navigate in different ways:

Person A: The Wanderer
He has no map, but is following the signs going east and knows he will eventually reach the signs that read New York City. This

is like the DIY person investing their money with their own researched information. They are attempting to follow the signs in front of them. When they are unsure of what to do next, they might ask directions. Since no actual strategy exists, this is the least efficient way to build wealth, in the same way it is the least efficient way to travel cross-country.

Person B: The Map Reader
This person has a physical map and is making decisions as to which routes to take through which cities. This is the person who uses a traditional financial advisor or a friend or family member to guide their investment decisions. Their information is based on someone else's experience. The map is correct in showing different routes, but does not take into account real time information. In the same way, your parent's advice could be outdated, your financial advisor could be biased, and your friend's advice could simply be completely wrong for you.

Person C: The GPS Follower
This person has a GPS that directs them in real time to the best route on their journey. This is very different from Person A and Person B because the changes in direction occur frequently. At each intersection, the GPS calculates which is the better direction to go, left or right, based on the traffic ahead. This is exactly what a DIP advisor is doing with your financial decision-making. They are calculating whether you are better off investing in real estate, the stock market, your student loans, a business opportunity, or perhaps something else. They are not biased in their recommendations, but are basing your next investment move on a series of different options that have been professionally analyzed. A person building their wealth will go much further using the DIP

strategy in the same way you will go further and faster using a GPS to navigate your journey.

Phase 2: Leveraging

After Phase 1, you should have grown some form of wealth, let's say $30,000. This might have been accumulated through dollar cost averaging with index funds. The DIP strategy would now have you analyze the next path to take. This could entail a 5% down payment on your own personal property, enabling a $600K purchase, or a 20% down payment for a $150,000 investment property. If your income qualifies you, and you are at the right stage of life, then this might be the very best use of your $30,000.

Should I put a 5% or 20% down payment on my home?

If you are renting a two-bedroom condo for $2500/m with a partner, and you have a down payment for the minimum 5%, you want to consider the advantages of buying now. For example, the Vancouver real estate market average home has appreciated by 9% each year since 2010. If you had a down payment of $30K, you could have bought a property for $600K. This would have been a small house or large townhouse. If you had taken another five years to have a 20% down payment of $120K, then yes, you would have saved on CMHC fees of approximately $22,800.

But, this fee could be added into your mortgage. Why would you pay this extra fee when you can simply save up more money? Well, after those five years, the $600K Vancouver property would cost you $923,174. So, your $120K down payment is no longer buying that same property at 20% down. Even worse, you have lost out on $323K in capital appreciation, and also not made the mortgage paydown over five years. If you are in a rapidly growing area, the capital appreciation growth should far

---

outweigh the CMHC fees. So, I believe you should always buy as early as possible whether with 5% or 20% down.

If I own a property when I am getting married, should I sell it if I need a larger place with my new partner?

This depends on your lifestyle trade-offs that you are willing to compromise. You will have a larger or better location if you sell, but you will likely have more equity in properties, and cash flow by not selling the first property. If you do decide to upgrade your home, you will have two options to buy your next home:

Option 1: You can sell the original property and have the tax-free equity for the down payment on your next home.

Option 2: You can leverage out the down payment using a HELOC, and keep the first property as a rental.

The first option is the most common, and easiest solution. Using the DIP strategy, Option 1 would be a last resort. A good cost-benefit analysis should be used to determine if you can afford the cash flow by holding both properties. If you need to hold off on RRSP or TFSA contributions, then the analysis will show whether in retirement you would be better off with one property plus RRSPs, or two properties without the RRSPs. You will likely be better off with two properties if they were in growing areas with low rental vacancy rates. If you cannot qualify for the two mortgages, then when you use Option 1, try to get a property that has a secondary suite to be rented out. This will reduce your overall expenses towards your home, while allowing for cash-flowing passive income to continue into retirement.

If you cannot find anything to buy, then the DIP strategy will just keep you investing monthly into your stock investments. However, this should not be too volatile of an investment because you are now on the lookout for a better alternative real estate investment that can be purchased at any time. This will include your own personal property, but should also include an investment property. A cash-flowing rental property will require a 20% down payment, but if you are in a high-priced area such as Metro Vancouver or the Greater Toronto Area (GTA), then you could look out of the province for a less expensive property. Real estate is the starting point to accelerating your wealth because you are able to take advantage of leveraged money. Essentially, you put a down payment (ex. 20%) and the bank puts in the remainder to buy the property. A renter pays down the mortgage over time. Over thirty years, you come to own the entire property that was paid down by the renter. You now have property that is worth millions, cash flows thousands, and can be passed onto the next generation. Many people have come to Canada, grown their wealth, and passed it onto their children using real estate.

> **Can I skip Phase 1, and still buy real estate?**
>
> Yes, possible. Are you comfortable with reaching out to joint venture partners? They can come up with the down payment, and you can work to find and manage the property. Are you comfortable with asking your parents or family member for the down payment? It might be an early inheritance or an investment partnership in a property. The advantage you have is buying yourself more time by starting earlier. The disadvantage is now being accountable to someone else besides yourself. If people you ask are not able to give you a down payment, ask if they have access to a line of credit (LOC), possibly from the equity of their home. You might use your monthly investment cash flow to simply service their LOC. With real estate, when an opportunity arises you need to get creative as to how you can take advantage of it.

Phase 3: Releveraging Equity

This is the phase where the growth really occurs. Unlike the stock investors, real estate investors typically leverage against their properties to reinvest their equity. This creates exponential growth since you now have more than one asset growing exponentially.

How does this work? If you have a property that is being paid off by a renter or a personal property that you are paying off, over time the value will go up and the mortgage will go down. The equity that you have accumulated can now be borrowed against from the bank, typically in the form of a secured line of credit, also known as a HELOC. You can now reinvest more into the stock market or more real estate.

The challenging part will be to determine if it is a good idea to take on more debt in order to reinvest. You will have interest accumulating against you each month, so the investment must yield a higher return to justify the added debt. When people are hesitant or risk averse, they tend to do nothing. This is what prevents them from breaking their wealth ceiling. A DIP advisor can help most at this juncture because he can do the analysis for you and determine if it is better to reinvest the leverage into the stock market, the real estate market, or possibly into a new business venture.

The DIP strategy is significantly different than what most investors are doing today. If you are investing a few hundred dollars each month into your RRSPs and TFSAs, then your money will grow at a slow pace over your lifetime. If you invest in leveraged assets such as real estate, then releverage periodically into more assets, your wealth will have an explosive growth that your traditional stock investments simply cannot compare to. Experienced investors are likely doing a form of the DIP strategy on their own already. However, the average person who wants to implement the strategy should get a DIP financial advisor to help them.

Chapter 4: The Secret Sauce of Investing

Do you like Kentucky Fried Chicken (KFC)? If so, why not make it at home? The answer: it is not the same taste when you try to do it on your own. KFC does not make their secret sauce public. The same applies to many other much-loved companies, including McDonald's or Coca-Cola.

Can you get consistent returns like Ray Dalio, the famous hedge fund manager? He started with nothing and is now one of the richest men in the US. He invests money for the planet's billionaires with one real goal in mind: preservation of capital.

He is well diversified—and this is very different from what traditional investors are doing now. They tend to have far too much stock exposure, which is why they ride the roller coaster of the stock market, with multiple years of negative returns. Dalio's formula, regardless of what the markets are doing, has consistent positive returns. For the wealthy, this is the most important goal with their passive investments.

Conversely, Warren Buffett has the majority of his assets in fewer than twelve stocks, with over 50% of them being in fewer than four stocks. This is their secret sauce to wealth for their clients.

However, at Latitude West, we are happy to share some of our real estate secret sauce. We do not aim to beat the stock market with our stock investments, but we do aim to get very high returns with our secret formula, which involves the integration and leveraging of real estate. Can you get these high returns on your own? Yes! But you would need your own secret sauce. I am going to reveal ours.

We look at three main components: cap rate, cash flow, and IRR.

- **Cap rate:** This is the ratio of net operating income of a property over the purchase price. To calculate on your own, simply subtract all the annual expenses from the total annual rental income generated, then divide by the purchase price. We do not take into account mortgage expense in our calculation; this is accounted for when calculating cash flow. We want properties with around 4% or higher cap rate, The higher the cap rate, the better. Between 4 and 8% would be ideal. When it gets higher than this range, investors need to be careful that the property is not in too challenging an area, or that the property will need a high capital expenditure in the near future.

- **Cash flow:** This is all of your monthly income minus all of your monthly expenses. Based on a 20% down payment, we would want to see a minimum breakeven or a positive cash flow. If the area will show great capital appreciation potential, we are also OK with a slightly negative cash flow. Remember, you can always increase a property's cash flow by putting more into the down payment. If an area is not cash flowing, we would want the property to have a growth rate of 5% or higher. This number might not be reflective of the area, but we would want it reflective of the property.

The property itself can have a higher growth rate due to the uniqueness of its location or the undervaluing of the property itself. We are flexible on some of these numbers, depending on the individual deal since the cap rate might be higher but with the cash flow lower (or vice versa in certain scenarios).

- **IRR:** This is the annual percentage return that investors most want to know about so they can compare with the alternative investments. For example, their stock investments might be yielding a 7% return, or the bank GICs might be giving a 3%. We can generate a projected IRR, the internal rate of return. This is similar to a return on investment (ROI), but it also takes into account the Net Present Value (NPV), which makes it more relevant. We aim for 12 to 22% IRR over a twenty-year period. Our unique analysis allows us to also show a projected IRR and cash return on a yearly basis. The IRR is our key number in helping us to compare the investment to alternative investment, including a stock investment.

Below is a sample of our analysis for an Airbnb condo with a $350K purchase price. Our assumptions are as follows:

- 3% value appreciation
- 30% vacancy rate
- 20% management fees
- 20% down payment
- 4.5% interest rate
- 30 year amortization
- Projected monthly rent $5018.75

If you are already a real estate investor, but have never had an Airbnb, you will notice the vacancy rate and management fee are much higher than long-term rentals. However, you will see by the projected annual rent why short-term rentals are now becoming popular.

First Year Expense Breakdown

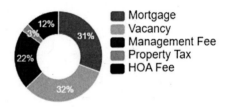

- Mortgage
- Vacancy
- Management Fee
- Property Tax
- HOA Fee

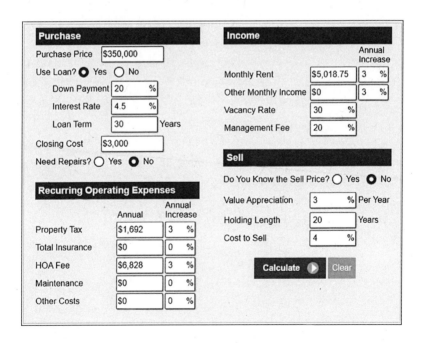

Purchase

Purchase Price	$350,000
Use Loan? ● Yes ○ No	
Down Payment	20 %
Interest Rate	4.5 %
Loan Term	30 Years
Closing Cost	$3,000
Need Repairs? ○ Yes ● No	

Recurring Operating Expenses

	Annual	Annual Increase
Property Tax	$1,692	3 %
Total Insurance	$0	0 %
HOA Fee	$6,828	3 %
Maintenance	$0	0 %
Other Costs	$0	0 %

Income

		Annual Increase
Monthly Rent	$5,018.75	3 %
Other Monthly Income	$0	3 %
Vacancy Rate	30 %	
Management Fee	20 %	

Sell

Do You Know the Sell Price? ○ Yes ● No

Value Appreciation	3 %	Per Year
Holding Length	20	Years
Cost to Sell	4 %	

Calculate ▶ Clear

As a result, our team is able to determine for this property the three metrics that guide all of our investment decisions with real estate:
- Cash flow $681.78 per month
- Cap rate of 7.2%
- An incredible internal rate of return of 19.58% annually, based on the sale of the property after 20 years

First Year Income and Expense

	Monthly	Annual
Income:	$5,018.75	$60,225.00
Mortgage Pay:	$1,418.72	$17,024.63
Vacancy (30%):	$1,505.63	$18,067.50
Management Fee (20%):	$702.63	$8,431.50
Property Tax:	$141.00	$1,692.00
HOA Fee:	$569.00	$6,828.00
Cash Flow:	**$681.78**	**$8,181.37**
Net Operating Income (NOI):	$2,100.50	$25,206.00

For the 20 Years Invested

Return (IRR):	19.58% per year
Total Profit when Sold:	$733,764.28
Cash on Cash Return:	1,005.16%
Capitalization Rate:	7.20%
Total Rental Income:	$906,230.25
Total Mortgage Payments:	$340,492.53
Total Expenses:	$228,935.59
Total Net Operating Income:	$677,294.66

Breakdown Over Time

Year	Annual Income	Mortgage	Expenses	Cash Flow	Cash on Cash Return	Equity Accumulated	If Sold at Year End	
							Cash to Receive	Return (IRR)
Begin				-$73,000				
1.	$33,726	$17,025	$8,520	$8,181	11.21%	$85,017	$70,597	7.92%
2.	$34,738	$17,025	$8,776	$8,938	12.24%	$100,557	$85,704	19.60%
3.	$35,780	$17,025	$9,039	$9,716	13.31%	$116,638	$101,339	22.53%
4.	$36,853	$17,025	$9,310	$10,519	14.41%	$133,280	$117,523	23.35%
5.	$37,959	$17,025	$9,589	$11,345	15.54%	$150,504	$134,274	23.44%
6.	$39,098	$17,025	$9,877	$12,196	16.71%	$168,331	$151,614	23.25%
7.	$40,271	$17,025	$10,173	$13,073	17.91%	$186,782	$169,564	22.94%
8.	$41,479	$17,025	$10,479	$13,976	19.14%	$205,882	$188,147	22.59%
9.	$42,723	$17,025	$10,793	$14,906	20.42%	$225,653	$207,386	22.24%
10.	$44,005	$17,025	$11,117	$15,863	21.73%	$246,120	$227,305	21.90%
11.	$45,325	$17,025	$11,450	$16,850	23.08%	$267,310	$247,930	21.57%
12.	$46,685	$17,025	$11,794	$17,866	24.47%	$289,247	$269,287	21.27%
13.	$48,085	$17,025	$12,147	$18,913	25.91%	$311,961	$291,402	20.99%
14.	$49,528	$17,025	$12,512	$19,991	27.39%	$335,480	$314,304	20.73%
15.	$51,014	$17,025	$12,887	$21,102	28.91%	$359,834	$338,022	20.50%
16.	$52,544	$17,025	$13,274	$22,246	30.47%	$385,053	$362,587	20.28%
17.	$54,120	$17,025	$13,672	$23,424	32.09%	$411,169	$388,030	20.08%
18.	$55,744	$17,025	$14,082	$24,637	33.75%	$438,218	$414,384	19.90%
19.	$57,416	$17,025	$14,505	$25,887	35.46%	$466,232	$441,683	19.73%
20.	$59,139	$17,025	$14,940	$497,136	37.22%	$495,248	$469,962	19.58%
Total	$906,230	$340,493	$228,936	$733,764	1,005.16%			

How can we get consistent double digits over a lifetime of investing over multiple assets? Now comes the second part of our formula. Unlike the stocks, our properties will create enough equity over time to be leveraged against. We devise a plan to leverage against the equity of the property in the future to buy even more real estate that fits these criteria. We then continue to do this as long as our clients can qualify for more mortgages and continue to believe in the philosophy. Over time, the mortgages will go down, the rents and equity will go up, and extraordinary wealth will be created.

This is how exponential wealth is created over a short period without depleting our client's current finances or retirement goals. Much like Ray Dalio's asset allocation, we have a secret sauce breakdown.

The DIP strategy consists of reserve, real estate, and stocks. When referring to stocks, this can include a stock/bond portfolio mix. With reserve, this is a combination of cash, fixed income such as GICs, and insurance-based investments. For real estate, we will have both passive and actively owned real estate. For the portfolio mix, reserve will fluctuate around 10 to 30%, with expected returns between 1 and 3%. This will give us our liquidity portion. Stocks will make up 20 to 50%, with a target between 6 and 8% returns. We do not want to take any large risks. We are looking for consistency and asset protection. Real estate makes up 30 to 70% and we're looking for 15 to 22% IRR over a 20-year period. This is the sector with large growth over long periods of time. It is where we must do the most work and get the most help. Because of the leverage used in this real estate portion, we are going to make the greatest returns. When first starting out, you want the stock portion to be higher because you can build wealth easily with vehicles such as TFSAs. But, over time you want the real estate portion to be the largest asset class. Below is a sample portfolio mix for a new investor in Year 1 with real estate making up only a third of their assets. Over time as real estate is prioritized using the DIP strategy, by Year 20, it now makes up the majority of the portfolio.

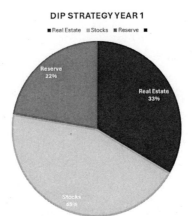

DIP STRATEGY YEAR 1

■ Real Estate ▩ Stocks ■ Reserve ■

Reserve
22%

Real Estate
33%

Stocks
45%

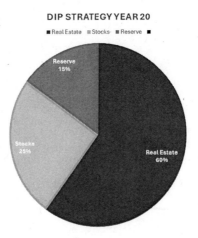

DIP STRATEGY YEAR 20

■ Real Estate ▩ Stocks ■ Reserve ■

Reserve
15%

Stocks
25%

Real Estate
60%

With this formula, can you do it on your own? The answer is maybe. It will not be hard for you to match the returns for the suggested reserve or stock portion. However, the most important ingredient of the secret sauce is the real estate. Finding a 4%+ cap rate based on a 20% down payment that breaks even or cash flows will be the novice investor's challenge. This means finding a property that is projected to grow 4 to 6%

consistently over twenty years, while cash flowing with changes in interest rates, vacancy rates, and growth rates.

Much like a stock hitting a home run, we have some properties making over a 30% return in the first two to three years due to the undervalued purchase price of the property alone. So, yes, you can do it on your own, but most people cannot, which is why it is easier, cheaper, and more time efficient to get a DIP advisor who specializes with real estate investors.

Can real estate agents fill the role of financial advisor? They are part of your financial team, but are not licensed to be your financial advisor. They will grow your wealth by helping you to buy real estate, but will not be projecting out your retirement plan. They are needed as a complement to a DIP advisor. A realtor will know the area well and could have inside information and accessibility for great properties. However, your realtor might be geographically limited by the location where they are licenced and live.

Can an accountant, mortgage broker, or lawyer fill the role? Usually it is far outside their expertise. They might give well-intended advice, but these professionals are unlikely to find you the property itself.

All of these professionals play an important role for your finances but should not be relied on beyond their field of expertise. In my experience, having a team to support your financial growth with an emphasis on real estate has worked out the best for the ordinary people who have created extraordinary wealth.

Chapter 5: Implementing the DIP Strategy

How can the middle class create eight figures of wealth in their lifetime without a side hustle? Dollar cost averaging 10% of your income is not going to get you there. We can also agree that other middle-income earners have gotten there. With my experience, I only know one possible way that does not involve large volatile risk. As this book has emphasized, it is in investing in real estate, then re-leveraging the equity after a few years to buy more. The strategy is not for everyone, but it is as simple as it sounds. Other strategies such as starting a business or day-trading in stocks have also resulted in creating an abundance of wealth, but for the average person, this is significantly more difficult than simply investing in real estate.

How can prioritizing the buying of your own home be used in the DIP strategy to grow wealth? If I buy my own home for $500K, and I use the minimum 5% down payment in Canada, then this is a $25K investment. Most Canadians can save this in a few years while in their twenties, or get this as a gift from parents. If the real estate value grows annually by 5% over the next five years, it will then be worth $638K in Year 5. The original mortgage of $475K will now be reduced to $471,850. The equity will be assessed by the bank as the market value of the home minus the remaining mortgage, which will be around $166K.

Now, if you were to qualify for an 80% loan on the equity, this would give you access to $132K in the form of a HELOC. You now go looking for another property on your own, or with a DIP advisor. If you can access $100K of your HELOC for the 20% down payment, you get another property for $400K. I advise you not use the entire HELOC since we want to keep some capacity for emergency expenses. You might need to transfer the HELOC money to your chequing account because the bank will want to see the source of your down payment and they will not like it coming directly from a HELOC. Leaving it in the chequing account for several months would be advisable. Remember, the interest of the HELOC will be tax deductible, an added bonus.

I am in my twenties, just starting to invest. How can I build wealth using the DIP strategy?

The first stage of wealth building is about accelerating your savings. If possible, lower your housing expenses by living with your parents. If that is not possible, get roommates. Dine out seldom, take local cheap vacations, and take transit or have an inexpensive used car.

Similar to a rocket trying to break Earth's gravity, all of your greatest efforts should be focussed at the beginning of your journey. You should put a minimum of 50% of your income into a TFSA with a conservative mix. You are not trying to hit a home run with this investment, just preserving capital and keeping up with inflation.

After a few years, when you have enough for a down payment, you should start looking for a property to live in. If still single, find a two-bed condo, and rent out the second room to a friend. Many people in their twenties are at a stage of life where they live with friends and enjoy the freedom of being single. Why not own the property and have the roommate pay down a portion of the mortgage while you gain the equity? Ensure the property has no rental restrictions in case you decide to keep the property after you have moved out.

By aggressively doing this initial wealth strategy in your early years, you will accelerate the time it takes for you to take advantage of any opportunity in real estate that arises.

The hard part of this strategy will be finding a property that is able to cash flow enough for the mortgage and the LOC. This would be a home run if you can find this. But, if you cannot, that does not mean you should not invest. Remember, there is nothing wrong with hitting a single or double in the game of real estate. This is where the right advisor comes in. A DIP advisor is able to assist in finding this property; as well, we are able to analyze the deal to ensure it is right for your long-term goals and your risk tolerance. Further, we can do a sensitivity analysis to ensure your probability of success is better than the other alternatives that you could do with your investment. Your wealth advisor should be able to do this analysis. If not, it may be worthwhile to add a real estate expert who is experienced in these strategies to your investment team. If you solely want someone to invest on your behalf in the stock market, then a traditional advisor will likely be the only person you need. But, if you believe that growing assets with real estate would expand your wealth beyond what you are doing now, then consider changing to a DIP advisor.

A Monte Carlo Analysis is a metric I used many times during my MBA. It is an analysis that will create a probability of success using a range of inputs for our sensitivity analysis. For example, we can say our RRSPs will grow at 5-10%/a over thirty years. Our Monte Carlo simulation will do 1000 samples of outcomes. We can then group the outcomes to see the probabilities of success. For example, our analysis might show that there is an 80% chance that our RRSPs will

> earn over $1M with those projected inputs. Conversely, with the real estate investments, we can do our Monte Carlo with the growth of the property at 2-4% growth rates if in a low appreciating area, such as the Prairies, or 4-8% rates if in a high appreciating area such as the GTA or Metro Vancouver. We can have rental increases from 1-5%/a. Using the same initial investment amounts, and applying our Monte Carlo, we can say that there is the same 80% chance that your real estate investment will be worth over $4M during the same time frame.

If the property was not able to cover all of the expenses, but it was a great property, then we can look at covering the shortfall with the monthly cash flow that you might typically invest in your RRSPs and TFSAs. The new property is bought for $400K, and we fund the shortfall for less than five years. This should be enough time for the mortgage to go down and rent to go up enough to break even. At the five-year mark, we look, once again, at how much HELOC we can take from the original property and the new property. We repeat and buy a third property. If you do this in your twenties or thirties, and continue to do so every five years, you should have at least three properties, not including your own home, by your forties and fifties.

At five properties, the banks will make it much harder for you to borrow. You can start getting creative with joint ventures then using a partner's capacity to lend. Or, just like *Monopoly*, you now want to start looking at multi-units. Commercial lending on multi-units is underwritten differently. Lenders look more closely at the building itself and its cash flow, as opposed to concentrating on you and your finances. Many people do not realize that for the investor who already owns five properties, in some cases it is actually easier to buy a twenty-unit building than it is to buy one extra unit.

If you still need convincing of the math analysis behind the DIP strategy, below is the total value of assets at retirement when comparing a strategy to buy three properties using a HELOC versus investing in traditional dollar cost averaging strategy. The top line represents the real estate assets. At Year 5 and Year 10, it jumps in value because a new property is bought. The bottom line represents the mortgage debt on the properties, which is why it jumps down in Year 5 and Year 10.

Real Estate Asset Summary

At Year 0, you will use $100K to buy a first rental property for $400K. Any cash flow from the property will be used as a reserve for expenditures. At Year 5, you will repeat the process by leveraging out $100K to buy a second rental property for $400K. The cash flow from the first property can be used to service the HELOC. Then in Year 10, you buy a third property again for $400K repeating the process. In this chart, we used properties with a 5% cap rate, a 4.5% interest rate, and conservatively increased the growth of the properties at only 3.5%/a.

We should now compare this with investing $100K in Year 0 into the stock market. In the graph above, the middle line represents a $100K investment into a balanced fund. With a 7%/a growth rate, it will be worth $386,968.45 in Year 20. With the three properties, the graph shows the value of the assets going up and the debts starting deeply in the negative. As time goes on, the debt increases up to zero around Year 40. In Year 20, the properties' asset values are $2,288,167, and the mortgage debts are $591,972. This will result in a net value of $1,696,194, which is over four times the value of the traditional stock investment strategy. In Year 35, around retirement age, this strategy shows the DIP strategy with assets of $6,098,252 and no more debts. The traditional stock strategy will only result in $1,067,658. How far will this amount go if your kids need help with a down payment, you have a long-term care need, or live a longer life than expected? The DIP strategy has created three extra cash-flowing properties, which results in six times greater net worth over the stock strategy.

Should you hire a property manager?

A property manager is used to manage a rental property for an investor. They will be responsible for finding and managing tenants, collecting rent, dealing with any issues. However, they typically come at a cost in the form of a monthly percentage of rental income collected. For example, if you charge $2000/m in rent, the property manager might charge 10%, thereby taking $200/m leaving you with $1800/m in income. There are three main reasons you might want to hire a property manager for your rental properties. First, it will enable you to focus on the career you are growing, and on the family you want to spend more time with. Second, a property management fee is tax-deductible, while your time and sweat equity are not. If you are a professional (ex. doctor, lawyer, engineer) managing your properties, the dollar per hour you are saving will not make sense compared to you using your time in your own profession. Last, and most important, by not managing your own properties it will enable you to scale out to buy more investments. The individuals who really break through their wealth ceiling tend to have five or more properties cash flowing. If you are managing all of these on a monthly basis, you will tap out quickly.

Do professional investors spend hours per week managing their rental properties? No. Once investors know what they are doing, management is more automated. A decision does need to be made every once in a while, such as a water heater needing replacement or a tenant moving out or requiring eviction. This is why I encourage my clients to hire a property manager once the time commitment gets to be too much. This might be on the first property or the fifth. For busy professionals with little interest or experience in managing a property, I typically tell them to bring on a property manager as soon as possible to "manage the toilets and tenants." Remember, the fees are only 5 to 10% of the rent and are tax deductible.

At four properties, my wife did not want me buying any additional because of the toll on my family, measured in time and headache. Once I brought on property managers, it was easier to scale out and focus any extra time in my month on buying more.

We want our clients to focus on their families and careers so my team and I show them properties that we have found to fit their criteria. We will have already incorporated a property management fee into the cash flow so they can see the numbers analyzed summarizing their cash flow and projected returns.

Chapter 6: The Need For Mentorship

"When the student is ready, the teacher appears." Lao Tzu

My uncle, my mother's younger brother, has always been a part of my life. One interesting fact—we have the same birthday, though he's twenty years older than I am. As a child, I knew him as a very, very scary man. My brother and cousins and I had stories of the odd ways he would discipline us. When I was in grade four, I still did not know my multiplication tables. Upon seeing my report card, he noticed there were many Cs. He was an engineer so he thought that it was unacceptable for me to be so poor in math.

One day, he decided to force me to learn the times tables. Of course, I was in complete panic. His decision may have been seen as a noble gesture, but for me, it resulted in pure fear. Still, I finally learned the times tables through hours of rote memorization and drills. The first day that I got a perfect score on my times table drill was more a day of relief than of thrill, just knowing that I had finally accomplished this task.

Little did I know what an effect learning my times tables at that age would have for me. Years later, I won the grade 10 math award for my school and in university, went on to earn my first degree in math. With this, I got my teaching accreditation, and teaching mathematics became my first career.

Aside from the igniting of my math career, I also received a financial education from my uncle. My father was in the insurance business, but realistically, he was a salesman, whether it was insurance, frozen foods, or cars. Unfortunately, my father never taught me anything about money, except for the importance of having it. When I was twenty-two years old, my mother encouraged me to connect with my uncle to buy a condo.

At the same time, Robert Kiyosaki's book *Rich Dad, Poor Dad* had a profound effect on me. He describes having a father who was not financially educated, and a friend's father, who was a wealthy hotel owner in Hawaii. Young Robert wanted to learn how to become wealthy. His father said, "I can't teach that to you. But your best friend Billy's father can." So he started to learn under the mentorship of Billy's father about how to create wealth, how to create a business, and how to become wealthy through real estate, mimicking the game of *Monopoly*.

As a recent university graduate, I did not understand much about investing in real estate. But my mother, whom I trusted, said I could make money learning from my uncle. He directed me to buy a $100,000 condominium with a 5% down payment. I did not know much about property investing, but I bought the condominium. It felt very grown up to own a property. My first renter was actually a girl I went to high school with.

Fast-forward three years: the leaky condo crisis hit British Columbia. This was caused by condos being built using the California-style stucco models. Unfortunately, we have significantly more rain than in California, and after a few years, the buildings started to leak. So now my $100,000 condo needed $18,000 in special assessment to fix the unit, money that I did not have.

This was my first grown-up investment gone wrong. Like

many novice investors, my first instinct was to try to sell it. Unfortunately, the market value of my condo was somewhere between $60,000 and $80,000. When I got my property assessment in the mail, it said my condo was worth $45,000. I was in crisis. What a mistake I had made!

When I started to do more research, I realized many people were trying to sell their condos, and I was now one of them. I felt that my uncle had swindled me. He had switched from his engineering career to becoming a real estate agent. I assumed he realized he could make more money investing in real estate than he could in engineering, but I felt that he had taken advantage of me.

When I met with him, I asked, "What should we do with this condo? How can I get out of this deal?"

He replied, "You are looking at this problem the wrong way. You should not be trying to sell your condo at a loss. Instead, you should be buying more condos at a discount."

"I can't even afford to pay the assessment—how am I going to buy more?" I whined.

This is what my uncle explained.

With real estate you always have options; you just need to explore them with the right advice. Option one: You can sell the condo, but you will take a loss on it. And since the mortgage is more than the value of the property, it will continue to cost you more, even after the property is sold. I did not like that idea at all.

Well, any other alternatives? Option two: You could get a line of credit. I had no idea what that even was so my uncle explained, "Finance the loss of the $18,000 and deduct the interest. Continue to rent it and hold on for dear life. The condo will eventually come back in value, and then focus on buying more." At that time, investors were allowed to put as little as 5% down payments on real estate. However, they were not allowed to put 5% down on a leaky condo.

My uncle further explained I shouldn't reinvest in my own building, but should rather pick up a condo that had already been fixed. Fixed buildings came with a ten-year warranty, and banks would lend on them. There was so much negativity toward condos, no one really wanted them because buyers had lost faith in the real estate market overall.

This is when I learned my second lesson: When everyone is running in one direction, look carefully at the other, and see if there is an opportunity. There is a famous investment quote, "When there is blood in the streets, buy." But, we should remember what the rest of the quote says: "even if it's your blood."

My opportunity was to buy fixed leaky condos for pennies on the dollar. There were significant discounts. Brand-new condos worth $140,000 were sold for $70,000. My uncle was picking up as many as he could get his hands on. He focused on the buildings he understood the most. And he developed a relationship with an overseas investor who had bought many of these condos and was now just trying to liquidate them.

I became interested in following his path to buy another one. He said that he was in the middle of closing on a deal, but another one just came across his desk. He would let me have it, but I would have to make my decision quickly. Luckily, with my math background I was able to analyze the cash flow. Based on a 5% down payment with the interest rate at around 6%, the property still cash flowed. It was a $140,000 condo, four years old, now selling for $104,000. A month prior, my uncle was picking up similar condos for $90K. Now the prices were trending back up.

At first, I thought maybe I was getting ripped off again

because he'd bought a similar one for $90K. Why couldn't I? He taught me another lesson in my flawed reasoning. Looking back at previous values is not the way you invest; you invest to make money. You let the numbers guide the decision, not the prior value. Otherwise, you would never buy real estate since all properties are valued at less if you look back far enough.

So, I took the leap and bought it. This turned out to be one of the best financial decisions I ever made. At the time, I was engaged, saving up for a wedding and a home for my future family. With my teacher's salary, I had enough for a 5% down payment on that property, but not enough for the $18K assessment. With my uncle's advice, I bought the property and financed the leaky condo assessment.

The next year when I married, the property was worth $143,000. Once the tides of the leaky condo debacle started to turn, the market slowly recovered back to intrinsic values. That next year, I sold the condo to use my equity as the down payment on my own home.

At that point, I was hooked. Real estate was a better way to create wealth. There was no way I could've saved up my $40K down payment in that one year using the stock market. I calculated that it would've taken me five years based on my teacher's salary to aggressively save the same amount.

The information and guidance I was receiving from my uncle was worth thousands. I was ready and eager to learn more. I talked to my uncle, desperate for more information about his strategies. I later learned that the majority of his wealth from real estate had been acquired during two separate periods: the 2008 financial collapse and the leaky condo crisis of the 1990s. This is when the greatest real estate opportunities had presented themselves, and he'd been able to capitalize on those opportunities.

By 2008, I owned several properties and was looking at other areas. I knew an opportunity existed—the US dollar was at par with the Canadian dollar, and the US was in the midst of a burst housing bubble. I did my research and narrowed down the opportunity to two different states: Arizona and Nevada. In hindsight, I would have been better off investing in Arizona. The only reason I chose to invest in Las Vegas was because the IRS allowed me to deduct trips that I would make to visit the property. At that time, I would rather have gone to Las Vegas than anywhere in Arizona.

At a dinner party, my uncle asked me about the areas I was looking at. I explained to him how I felt the US, specifically Las Vegas, was geared to do well. He took my information and moved to Las Vegas for a few months because he was retired by that time. Over the course of three months he was able to buy multiple condos and houses for pennies on the dollar. The main advantage he had was cash because US lenders were no longer lending to Canadians like him and me. His second advantage was that he already owned real estate, and Canadian banks were allowing him to use a HELOC. His final advantage was time. He had those few months to learn the market and learn the areas, so he already knew the intrinsic value of the property when I arrived. I bought one property, while he had bought six. I liked the diversification of buying property in the US because I envisioned using the US dollars in my retirement as my vacation cash.

Two years after he bought all those properties, the US dollar started to pull away from the Canadian dollar, and the properties' value increased dramatically. He doubled almost all of his investments within two years. To date, he nets over $60,000US annually on his Vegas properties, which he uses to vacation around the world. I calculated that, based on my uncle's income, there is no way he could have built this same wealth with passive income in the stock market.

That's how my uncle became a mentor and a guide. I realized that even though his advice went against conventional wisdom, even against my parents' advice at times, he was the only rich person I knew willing to advise me.

Three Regrets of Real Estate Investing

If you have a friend or family member who has invested in real estate and made money, you will be very familiar with the Three Regrets of Real Estate.

Regret 1: Not investing earlier

Here in the Vancouver area, there are countless stories of people who can no longer afford to buy a property in the city they love, and are now caught with the ever-increasing high rental cycle. They have no equity in property, they have kids, and have even greater housing needs. They likely had the opportunity to buy over ten years ago, but passed on the opportunity. Potentially they used excuses like the market is too high, or a higher down payment would be better, or they would be better off renting and investing in the stock market. These people who have fallen into Regret 1 today are sleeping like babies...they are waking up every two hours and crying.

Regret 2: Not buying more

I experienced this regret after I bought that two-bed condo in the US in 2008 for $80K. I only needed to put $16K down payment, which was taken from a Canadian HELOC. However, I intended to buy three condos using my extra funds and access to my line of credit. After I bought the first one, the US market continued to go down. I made the

---

mistake of listening to others who thought I was taking on too much risk by buying anything at all in the US at that time.

They used words like "I would never do that," "You are crazy," or "Just stick to one and see how it goes." When the market kept going down, they said, "Aren't you glad you didn't buy more?" I've told my clients many times: the most dangerous financial advice you can receive is from family and friends who have no experience. No analysis was ever conducted by the people commenting on my financial decision. They were giving their opinion, which was biased to their lack of investing experience. If I would have stuck to my plan, I would have another $650KUS by retirement, with $36,000US per year of passive cash flow.

Regret 3: Selling too early

I had a client whose parents owned a large property in Vancouver. When they retired, they wanted to utilize the equity in their home. They sold their house for roughly $4M in 2010. They downsized to a very nice condo that cost $1M. When I spoke to the father a few years later at a dinner party, I asked how retirement was going.

"Great," he said.

I knew he was well off, and was a smart businessman, so I also asked, "Any advice for when I retire?"

He said there was only one great regret. "I never should have sold my house." At the time, he thought the market was at an all-time high in Vancouver, and he was getting top dollar for this home. It was waterfront with an unobstructed view. He had paid less than a $1M over twenty years earlier. He said today it would be worth over $10M.

When he retired, he was still young enough to golf, travel, and be active in his grandkids' lives. Being in business, he surely understood money and finances, but was he getting the right financial advice? Or worse, was he trying to do it himself?

I was not his financial advisor, but if I had been, we would have run a Monte Carlo analysis on the probability of success over putting the equity into the stock market, or keeping the real estate. The option to downsize still would have been there, but selling is what we would have been analyzing to determine if it was the best option.

Regardless, our data in 2010 would have been similar to the data of today. Metro Vancouver still does not have enough supply to accommodate the next fifteen years of predicted immigration and housing demand. The next decade, as with the last decade, should still show housing prices continuing to increase. If he had the right advice, selling should have been a very last option in retirement. The use of a DIP advisor could have saved him millions.

Chapter 7: The Information Gap

"Some men see things as they are and say why. I dream things that never were and say why not." Senator Robert Kennedy

You've heard the saying, "The rich are getting richer."

The response question should be, "What are they doing that I am not?"

The answer is very simple: They are investing better than you are. Why? They have better information.

In 2010, I volunteered in Central America as a team leader with a small group. On one leg of the flight to our destination, I was fortunate enough to be bumped into first class and was seated beside a man with whom I sparked a conversation that turned out to be enlightening. Coincidently, we had one commonality: we both had bad feet. Since he knew I would be volunteering, which included much walking, he was interested in the type of shoes I wore. In return, he was kind enough to humour me with conversation.

He was on his way to the World Cup in South Africa for which he had tickets, each ranging in price from $10,000 to $20,000, for friends and family members. He was going to multiple games. I realized the magnitude of his wealth. He later told me that he owned a major hotel in Whistler, B.C., and had several holdings around the US.

The conversation moved toward his children. All had graduated from an Ivy League school, and he was a board member in the business school at that university. The fascinating thing was that he did not come from wealth. When he was young, he drove a cab at night and put himself through college. He worked in the energy sector, started his own company, and made his first million by age thirty.

I could tell he was an outside-the-box thinker, typical for self-made entrepreneurs. He had written a book in which he shared all the secrets he wanted to pass on but he only made eleven copies of the book and shared them with specific people, including his three children, his nieces, and his nephews. He never sold the book or made it public. This, in essence, demonstrates the ultimate gap in wealth. It is the information gap between the rich and the poor.

Ancient Talmud Philosophy: The First Balanced Portfolio

I started this book by telling an immigrant story of my mother and her siblings. A well-known testament to the immigrant success story is that of the Jews. When they immigrated to the US, they were often penniless. They first came at a time when English as a second language instruction was not being offered in schools, and there was a racial bias against them. Today they are one of the most disproportionately wealthy cultures in the US. Rabbi Daniel Lapin, who has a background in Mathematics and Economics, has written a number of books, two of which are *Thou Shall Prosper: The 10 Commandments for Making Money* and *Business Secrets from the Bible: Spiritual Success Strategies for Financial Abundance*. In these books and in his podcasts, he examines the reasons for this prosperity, tracing it back to the Talmud.

The Talmud, which dates back to 200-500 CE, is a discussion of the teachings of the Torah, the Jewish Books of the Law, which try to both understand how the teachings apply and to seek answers for the situations that rabbis were encountering. From this text, Lapin derives principles, the following of which, he argues, can lead to a healthy, wealthy, and faithful life. He notes that people who identify as Jewish form as little as 1.7% of the American population, yet they comprise approximately 30% of the Forbes 100 wealthiest people in America. In *Thou Shall Prosper* he tackles the question: "Why are Jews disproportionately wealthy?"

He fights against the stereotypes of Jews and instead addresses how their sacred teachings explain what they ought to do with their money. That teaching provides not only a prescription for wealth, but also for happiness and generosity, the two aspirations not being mutually exclusive. It involves principles for investing money while also being charitable, and taking time to rest from business and work. The asset allocation it recommends has been referred to as the first balanced portfolio in history.

What is the secret balanced portfolio that has resulted in centuries of wealth wisdom from the Talmud? Lapin explains how the Talmud teaches how to allocate money. It is a basic formula, but do not dismiss its magnitude due to its simplicity. Its recommendation for all investors is to divide wealth into thirds: business, land, and reserve. If we translate this into today's modern investments, we would say business could be your own business or someone else's business. For the average person today without a business, this would be the stock market. For land, this would be real estate, ideally, cash-flowing real estate, which is why I would not count your home in this category, but only rental real estate. Although your home is an asset that grows in value over time, it generates no cash flow, nor is it meant to be sold at a later date. If you were to sell it, you would still need to live somewhere else, in which case you would likely need the equity to buy again.

Finally, the last category is reserve, a harder one for people to understand. Why would you need a third of your wealth not making any money? We need liquid assets such as cash in case of an emergency. Today we can invest in insurance to achieve a similar goal. In ancient times, gold was their version of cash because it was a liquid store of value. This asset class more importantly can be used in case there is a major opportunity in either business or real estate.

Here is an example of how this can work. Those with all of their money in a crashed market, such as occurred in 2008 or 2020, had no real opportunity to invest in a stock market that was down over 25%. Statistically, these markets recover within two years, on average regaining all losses. This is a double-digit return for any new money invested. In 2008, the US housing market had crashed, and property in multiple states was down over 50%. The cost to rebuild some of these properties was higher than what the properties were being sold for. As well, the Canadian dollar was at par. With reserve, and a financial advisor who understood the value of investing in property, both my uncle and I took advantage of this opportunity.

My clients in 2020 with reserve also took advantage, and accelerated their wealth with leverage. Our team was able to understand the opportunity with a Monte Carlo analysis. We predicted a double-digit ROI over a three-to five-year period with new leveraged money, with interest rates on the money at approximately 4%. Our clients got their double-digit returns in under one year due to the Covid crisis recovery. You might be thinking, "I can also leverage new money with my stocks," but I would not be comfortable recommending this with any of my clients, nor should you. If the stocks were to go down even further, you will have both new and old stocks go down. And, a margin call will not help your sleepless night situation.

Those with all of their money in a stock balanced portfolio were likely stressed, with their advisors telling them to stay the course, not to panic, and keep dollar cost averaging. Popular self-made investors like Robert Kiyosaki and Grant Cardone have said they love crashed markets, either stock or real estate, because they make more money in those times. Why not you?

> **To hear more about the Talmud explanation, YouTube "The Talmud Portfolio | Ancient Investing Wisdom versus Modern Portfolio Theory"**

For my own three girls, I started passing on my own wealth formulas when they were very young, beginning with the popular three-jars method. When they were seven, their allowance was based on their age, so the seven-year-old would make $7 per week. This would be tied to chores around the house. At the end of the week, a third went into savings, which they would never spend but instead watch it physically grow because I paid them in coins. A third went to charity so they would understand the importance of giving back, and only one-third was for spending, with which I would allow them quite a bit of freedom so they could learn from their mistakes.

When they turn eighteen, they will all open up a TFSA and an FHSA (First Home Savings Account) investment account. I do not want to fully control their money but rather I'll give them latitude to have their own successes and mistakes. Yes, dollar cost averaging is how they will start off, but this will be short-lived. By the time they finish some form of postsecondary education, real estate will become our focus. If they decide to follow their passion, which leads them to a career with a low wealth ceiling, then it will be even more important that they implement information I pass on about growing wealth.

Parents are bonded by one universal truth: We love our kids, and we want them to be happy and successful. However, how they are taught about money tends to be the major factor in whether they go up a notch, down a notch, or stay at the same financial level as the generation before them. I know many cases of wealthy families where their children have gone down in comparison to their parents. In my case, I have gone up a notch due to higher education, but more importantly thanks to having better financial information.

A parent is the main source of financial information for most people. The better the information that the parents pass down to the next generation, the higher the probability that their children will go up a notch in wealth. Sometimes this information means not making the same financial mistakes as their parents made. Other times this information shares the secrets of how parents acquired their wealth. Enabling children to implement these secrets at an early age provides more time for them to grow their wealth.

The key factor in going beyond my personal wealth ceiling was that I implemented information my uncle passed on to me starting in my early 20s, which involved the investment of real estate. Who is passing on their wealth secrets to you?

Chapter 8: How the Rich Invest Differently Than You

Most people will agree that if you want to improve any area of your life, then a first step is to see what the experts are doing then try to model their formula for success. We are already doing this when we cook with a new recipe, start a new exercise regime, or start a new job. Our investments should be no different. However, when it comes to investing, people should ask, "Why are we not getting rich? If we are looking to expert advice to increase our wealth status, why are the experts not getting us there?"

The answer: we get average returns with our investments because we model middle-class investment strategies. This keeps us in the middle class and far below our wealth ceiling. To break our wealth ceiling, a starting point would be to look not at individuals, but instead to those institutions that are already rich.

How are these groups getting outstanding consistent returns? Let's start with the Tiger 21. This is a peer-to-peer group of investors who are some of the wealthiest people on the planet. The minimum amount of wealth needed to be a part of the group is $10 million of investable assets and the average investor has approximately $80 million in assets. These are typically people who have sold companies and need the best advice on how to preserve and grow the wealth. It is just as important for us to examine what they do not do as it is to see what they do with their investments.

There are things they definitely do not do: hand their money over to an adviser who creates an 80/20 portfolio of stock/bonds taking 2% MER fees. They do not do DIY dollar cost averaging in index funds. Consider this: the Tiger 21 hold only 25% in public stocks, 27% in real estate, 22% in cash, and the remainder in other asset pools. If they make above-average S&P 500 benchmark returns, then at least one of these asset classes must be having outstanding returns. Which of these three asset classes do you think is pulling up the ROI average the most? Yes, the real estate, both passive and active real estate. The passive real estate has the investors investing in real estate that another institution is buying and selling. The active real estate is physical properties that the investors are purchasing themselves, which might include residential housing, commercial, retail, or land developments.

The average investor relies too heavily on stocks in their portfolio. When the markets are down, they are stressed, not sleeping well at night. The Tiger 21 has stock exposure, not stock reliance. When the markets are down, less than a third of their portfolio has been affected. Further, when the markets are down, the average investor cannot do anything but wait for the markets to recover so they cannot take advantage of buying the good stocks that are available. Conversely, much like the Talmud strategy, the Tiger 21 will have two asset classes to capitalize on the down market: cash and real estate. The cash is liquid and can be utilized to buy the cheap stocks immediately. Further, they can use their real estate to also take advantage of "on sale" markets. Unlike a stock portfolio, real estate can be leveraged against to pull money out through the HELOC. Further, the interest on the leveraged money would be tax deductible.

The second group for us to examine is institutions that are responsible for large pension funds. These funds are in the billions, and are responsible for preserving wealth as well as growing it consistently. Forbes released an article entitled "Why Large Pension Funds Are Investing in Private Real Estate" by Kellie Rastegar. The study showed how 30% of large institutions want to increase their private real estate exposure. In the past, institutions that wanted real estate exposure without direct ownership would invest in Real Estate Investment Trusts (REITs). However, these institutions are now leaning against REITs and are shifting towards private real estate. REIT dividends are commonly taxed higher than stock dividends, and REITs are highly sensitive to both the stock market and interest rate fluctuations. Large institutions like private real estate for another reason. The institutions have greater control and influence over each deal. This can include the property management, maintenance, lease agreements, and the purchase price. "As a result of this dedicated supervision, returns from private real estate can range between 15%-20%, three to five points above those earned in public markets. Unsurprisingly, private equity now constitutes over 25% of the average institutional investor's portfolio."

Investing in Private Real Estate

With the DIP strategy, the average individual investor can model what the wealthy are already doing. In no other time in history has it been easier to access the information of what the wealthy are doing with their money. I advise: Follow their money, follow their trends, follow their portfolio, and your wealth will follow theirs.

Does my personal home count as being invested in private real estate?

Typically no. However, if you are renting a portion of your home, or intend to downsize and cash out the equity, only then would I include that portion as the investment in this category. For the REITs, most will not get you double-digit returns for your overall portfolio, and you cannot enjoy the tax deductions or the leveraged opportunities. By investing in REITs, you will likely get somewhere between 6-9% returns, but it will not be strong enough for your portfolio overall to get returns to break your wealth ceiling, which is the goal of the advice in this book.

Chapter 9: The Five-to-One Rule of Real Estate

Many people do not fully understand how wealth accelerates at an exponential level when investing in real estate over the long term.

When you invest $100,000 in the stock market and receive a 10% ROI, this would be a $110,000 return after one year. When you invest in real estate with the same $100,000, you are typically not buying a $100,000 asset. Investors are buying rental property, where the $100,000 represents the down payment of 20%. This down payment of $100,000 will enable you to buy a $500,000 property, as long as the bank qualifies you. If the $500,000 property goes up by 10% in one year, then the property is now worth $550,000. When you measure the real ROI, it is based on a $50,000 gain on the $100,000 down payment because that is the only amount you invested. Therefore, you have actually increased your ROI by 50%.

This, in essence, is the five-to-one rule. In real estate with a 20% down payment, you are going up 5% every time the asset goes up by 1%. With this same logic, if you invest a 10% down payment, then for every 1% increase in asset value, you go up by 10%. That explains how real estate investors we are getting double-digit or even greater returns.

Infinite Returns

When I first heard Robert Kiyosaki explain how he gets infinite returns, as a former Calculus teacher I was intrigued. I'll explain what I learned.

Consider an example of a $100K investment with a 10% return annually, or $10K. If you were to achieve the same $10K with only a $50K investment, you would have had a 20% return. If you were to achieve the same $10K with a $25K investment, then you would have had a 40% return. If we follow the pattern of lowering the investment but keeping the $10K return constant, we would have the return approaching infinity, hence the term "infinite returns."

This is mathematically accurate. Take my $350K Abbotsford house. If I invested $50K to buy the house in year one, then in year six, I leveraged out the $50K in the form of a Home Equity Line of Credit (HELOC) to reinvest elsewhere, I would then have none of my original money in the Abbotsford house. The cash flow is enough to cover the mortgage, taxes, HELOC interest, and any other expenses, including the property management fees, which means the property is not taking up any of my time, nor any more of my money. In fact, it is giving me annual cash flow that is now infinite.

In summary, I have learned, through my studying of what the wealthy do, to not only invest in cash-flowing assets, but to reinvest and create infinitely returning cash-flowing assets. This strategy is not limited to the ultra-wealthy nor to large institutions, but is available to all average Canadians.

You cannot use this strategy with stocks. Or more correctly, you should not do this with stocks. It is just too risky for an average investor to leverage against their stocks. Which financial advisor would recommend you leverage against your kids' RESPs or your RRSPs?

Simply put, average-income investors I know have accumulated the bulk of their wealth through investing in real estate, then re-investing the equity in more real estate.

There are several other factors to consider when comparing stock investment to real estate. First, the exit costs for the real estate will be different from stocks. There will be real estate agent fees, legal fees, and possibly other expenditures to sell the property. As well, consider the city, the neighbourhood, and the type of real estate. This will affect the projected growth rate. If I used a 5% growth rate, some people might say that that number is too high for a rural area in Manitoba. Conversely, in the Lower Mainland of Vancouver or the GTA, this number might be considered too low.

If we use the Canadian housing average of 6.2%, this still achieves double-digit growth after exit fees over twenty years. Conversely, if the property goes down in value, are we not also getting double-digit losses? The quick answer is yes. But just like any other investment, you have not lost or gained anything until you have sold it. This is why you have often heard that real estate is an investment in the long game.

Below is the Greater Vancouver Housing Prices from 1977 to 2023. It shows the benchmark average home price in the Lower Mainland to be $1,210,000 (July 2023) whereas in 1977 it was $80,000. This is an annual average growth of 6.37%.

Vancouver Real Estate History Prices

The asset/liability comparison below compares the long-term value of a $100K investment in the stock market growing at 7% annually with the same investment in real estate, with a $100K down payment for a $500K property growing at 6% annually.

Option 1: Stocks

	Rates	Initial Investment		Year 1	Year 20	Year 30	Annual Return on Investment
Stock		$100,000	Asset	$100,000	$396,968	$761,225	
Growth Rate	7%		Liability	$0	$0	$0	
			Equity	$100,000	$396,968	**$761,225**	**7%**

Option 2: Real Estate

	Rates	Initial Investment		Year 1	Year 20	Year 30	Annual Return on Investment
Real Estate		$100,000	Asset	$500,000	$1,603,567	$2,871,745	
Growth Rate	6%		Liability	$400,000	$195,559	$0	
Mortgage Rate	4.5%		Equity	$100,000	$1,408,008	**$2,871,745**	**12%**

At 6% growth, the property after thirty years is now worth $2,871,745, compared to the stock asset that is only $761,225. For the stock to match the investment, it would have needed to achieve a 12% annual average over the same thirty-year time frame. For the average investor, this is almost an impossible task. For a real estate investor, this is a basic investment. With real estate, however, the downside is that there are other recurring costs and hassles to consider: renters, capital expenditures, real estate agent fees, legal fees, and the time required to manage, find deals, and handle problems. Is an extra $1M+ worth the hassle? I believe the answer is yes.

Further, the rent that can be seen as a cash-flowing dividend arriving monthly. If an experienced real estate investor can get the rental income to cover the property taxes, mortgage payments, management fees, and other expenses then the cash flow will only be break even. This is not a bad thing. A 20%

down payment is ideal, but today in areas such as Vancouver and Toronto, this is almost impossible. However a DIP advisor should be able to find you an investment that will fit the criteria in various other markets.

For real estate investors, rent is considered equivalent to an annual stock dividend. However, unlike dividends, the cash flow from rent will increase significantly over time. This is because you have two numbers going in the right direction—rent, which increases with the inflation of the rental market, and the mortgage, which decreases each month as the renter pays it down.

Historically, Canadian rent has increased 1 to 5% annually, depending on the housing market you are in. Vancouver and Toronto rental rates have increased much more than the Canadian average. In 2009, the average two-bedroom condo rented in Vancouver for $1061/m. In 2022, the same condo rented for $1900/m. This is an annual growth rate of 4.6%.

Rent Residential Real Estate Vancouver

The longer you hold a property, the more rent you will receive. Using the sample two-bedroom property above that was purchased for $500K, the table below shows the rent projected in Metro Vancouver over the next forty years.

	Growth rate	Year 1	Year 20	Year 30	Year 40
Rent	3%	$1900/m	$3431/m	$4611/m	6198/m

If the rental rate in this area grew by 3% per year, then in Year 30, the rent would be $4611/m, but the mortgage would be gone. The expenses would only be a minor fraction of the rent. So, $3000/m income should easily be netted for this one property. Now consider using the DIP strategy and retiring with five or more similar properties.

We already see Canadians taking on extra shifts at work, second jobs, or a side hustle just to get a little further ahead. Most of these will not be equivalent to an extra $1M in retirement assets and thousands in monthly cash flow. Of course, real estate will require some extra hours each month, but nothing like an extra job would require. As well, with the right team of property managers, contractors, mortgage brokers, real estate agents, and of course, a DIP financial advisor, the extra work is minimized, and worth the effort.

Chap 10: The Top Three Advantages of Investment Real Estate

Investment real estate has three main advantages over mutual funds, stocks, and bonds.

First, there is the tax advantage. You can deduct the mortgage interest on your income tax. This will reduce your taxable employment income, and can help to offset any negative cash flow from the rental property. You can deduct any additional expenses attached to this property. If you upgrade the kitchen, or create a rental suite, these costs are adding value to the property on resale, and will help to increase the rental cash flow, but at the same time these are counted as tax deductions. If you use borrowed money for these expenses, the interest too is deductible. As well, even if the property increases in value, you can depreciate the property on your tax return thereby lowering your income taxes while your wealth increases.

Second, real estate is a leveraged asset, unless you buy it outright, which I do not encourage. The leverage component will accelerate the equity returns, as the Five to One Rule shows. But even more importantly, the equity from the real estate can be leveraged back out with a home equity line of credit (HELOC) strategy to buy even more real estate. You cannot do this with stocks or bonds, and if you tried, it could not be done at the same degree or the same risk levels.

Third, investment properties, over time, will cash flow.

This is a bold statement, I know. People will have stories of properties they own that are not cash flowing. All investments come with risk, but we can all agree that better information produces better returns. If the property has been analyzed correctly, it will dramatically minimize the risk of it being cash flow negative. If it is negative to start, the fundamentals of real estate show that two numbers affecting your cash flow will be going in the right direction. The mortgage, which is paid by your renter, over time continues to go down, and rent, which is charged to your renter, over time continues to go up. In retirement this cash flow will replace your income. After you pass away, this non-depleting income will be passed onto your spouse, then onto your kids.

Finally, with real estate, you have the opportunity to be at an information advantage. Your realtor, who knows property well, can let you know if there is a distressed seller. The city plans can show that a hospital is being built near the property within the next few years. The house might have the ability to be converted into two suites with a $30K capital investment. These will all increase the value of the property more than the overall area's rate of increase. Knowing how you personally can add value to the property is a competitive advantage that you do not have in the stock market. Your only advantage with stocks is the research that you find, but not any form of value that you can add once the stock is purchased.

Unfortunately, the problem with investing solely in stocks is your information disadvantage. With any individual stock or sector, there are two many large players who have more information than you. The buying and selling of stocks is a zero sum game. They will know at what price point the stock will make sense to buy and the price point at which the stock should be sold. Institutions will have teams of professionals with finance and economic degrees, which you do not. For an average Canadian investor, buying and selling stocks should be nothing more than a side interest with a minimal amount of money, like sports betting or a night at the casino. It should never be with any real detrimental amount. You really will not know if you are buying at a high or low or what its future value is going to be. You are risking too much on your ability to outperform individuals who have been professionally trained. To put this in perspective, even if you work out at your local gym, would you ever challenge an MMA fighter to a few rounds?

If you feel that you do not have the time or expertise to find or add value to any investment real estate, then perhaps you are working with the wrong advisors. For our clients at Latitude West, we help to find these undervalued areas, and advise them in adding value. There might be a few competitors, which is why we can also calculate the purchase price point at which the property will make sense to buy. For a stock investor, they will be bidding on a price point with thousands of others looking at the buy and sell point of that stock at any given moment. For a property there is only one seller, and a handful of potential buyers looking at any given time. They odds are in your favor with real estate, and the probability of success much higher.

Do stocks have the ability to lose 20%, 50%, even 100%? Unfortunately yes. Conversely, I have yet to find a Canadian property that has been worth less than its original value after twenty years. This also applies to the ability to rent it out. If it is priced correctly at fair market value, most property should be able to be consistently rented with around a 3-5% vacancy rate, and rent should be appreciating with inflation at 1-3% annually, and it will be higher in more desirable, low-inventory cities.

The financial planning industry tends to fall short in helping people to achieve through both stock and real estate. Stocks are still an excellent vehicle to grow wealth, but should not be your only vehicle, and will not be the way to breaking your wealth ceiling. Our team at Latitude West gives both real estate and stock advice showing how the two are most effective when used together. By charging a fee-for-service, my team and I can leverage our strengths of analyzing opportunities to invest in, and comparing with various asset classes. This includes not only traditional stocks, bonds and GICs, but also investment real estate. All Canadians work hard for their money, and should want more from their investment options.

Should I invest for Cash Flow Versus Capital Appreciation?

"Ships are most safe in the harbour. But, that is not what they were built for."

Should you invest for cash flow or capital appreciation? Most investors will tell you to invest for cash flow first, and have capital appreciation be the bonus. But, what if you cannot find a cash-flowing property? Are you going to not invest at all and let years of potential real estate investing pass you by? I believe you should always be investing in real estate, and when you have your down payment and finances ready for the next buy, you should simply buy the best deal at the time. You do not have to hit a home run with every real estate deal. A single or double base hit is completely fine. The properties I have invested in for capital appreciation have done fine, and eventually cash flowed. The properties I have invested in for cash flow have eventually appreciated in value.

Should you invest in a negative cash-flowing property? Maybe. The Lower Mainland and the Fraser Valley, for example, have shown a capital appreciation that has beat the Canadian average. We have low supply for the high demand but our prices are also among the highest in Canada. When my clients ask me whether it is a good idea to buy investment property in the Lower Mainland, I always answer, "Maybe." It depends on the property, the rents, the lending rate, the projected value appreciation, etc. In most cases, it will also likely be negative cash flow based on a 20% down payment.

However, if you have invested in a high appreciating area such as Metro Vancouver or the GTA in the last twenty years, you have likely made $100K or more in a short time. There are two ways to make the investment work in an area like Vancouver. First, you can simply make a larger down payment. To get a property to cash flow in Vancouver, typically 35-50% would be needed. Or, you can use your own personal monthly cash flow and make up the shortfall. This would be your RRSP monthly contribution equivalent as described already. But the question remains: Is this a good idea? This is where people get stuck, and this is why a non-biased DIP advisor who knows how to analyze real estate is needed. An average non-cash-flowing real estate investment should be cash flowing within five years if analyzed correctly.

Chapter 11: How Our Kids Will Be Able to Afford a Home in Canada

When we first have kids, we are both excited and scared. We worry about them the day they are born, and it never ends regardless of their age. Often, the first financial concern is how you are going to save up for their education. Friends and family will tell you to set up an RESP for them through the bank or a financial advisor. However, a child's education will likely not be the big financial difficulty they face. With the unaffordable price of housing, the larger problem will be how they can one day buy a home.

I have a client who, wanting to buy her first place, is getting help from her parents. She has a university degree with a professional job making under $60K annually, and she wants to stop renting, which her parents are encouraging. After meeting with the mortgage broker, she discovered that she qualifies for less than $300K of mortgage. She lives and works in Metro Vancouver, and wants to stay in the area because her family, friends, job, and life are all there. Unfortunately, there is absolutely nothing she can buy with this amount of mortgage and her down payment. Fortunately, her parents are going to help with an incredible $450K down payment. Unfortunately, they will be using an LOC from their home to do so, and will be servicing the interest themselves.

How much of an impact will this have on their retirement? Will they be able to service this LOC for another thirty years, or will they pass the expense onto their adult child eventually? What is more shocking is that even with this $700K budget, she can only afford a one-bedroom condo in her area of Vancouver. What will happen if she is to marry and wants to upgrade to a larger home? We now have an educated professional living in a small condo, with loving parents taking on a massive financial expense just to keep their daughter in the city close to them. However, she may be one of the lucky ones. At least she will be an owner, not a renter, living in the area of her choice.

I have recently had two client couples move to the Prairies from Metro Vancouver due to housing. They could not afford to buy anything locally, nor could they afford to upgrade their condo to a larger home. We are seeing other friends and family members move out of province in order to buy more suitable housing. I do not blame them because they are doing what is best for their families. However, for new parents, we should be asking ourselves how we can prevent this from happening to their children when they get older. This is the crisis for people in unaffordable Canadian cities.

The days of go to school, get good grades, get a decent job, get married, buy a nice home and start a family are not a reality for many young Canadians. Those times are long gone, especially in areas such as Metro Vancouver and the GTA. We now find that couples are delaying getting married in order to save up for a down payment, or are delaying having kids in order to try to buy a house. The means they are marrying later in life, having fewer kids, and struggling to buy. Delaying marriage often puts a strain on relationships. Having fewer kids causes our society to increase taxes, since it is relying more on a limited population. But the larger implication for buying a home later in life is the loss in capital appreciation. A person who owns a home from age twenty-five to sixty-five will typically have close to double the home equity at retirement compared to someone who only owns from age thirty-five to sixty-five. To show numerically, if you bought a $500K home growing at 6%, it would be worth $5,142,859 in 40 years. The same home would be worth $2,871,746 after 30 years. The extra ten years of owning the property would give you another $2,271,113 in equity. In Canada, this is tax-free capital gains. By helping our kids to buy a home as early as possible, we are also helping them to marry, start a family, live closer to us, and retire on their terms without being victim to their financial situation.

Is there a solution? I believe if we start early enough we can avoid many of the problems described. But it will take real estate to solve the problem of real estate. Buying investment real estate for your child under your name will likely solve this pending problem, but only if you have enough years to invest. As a DIP advisor, I would be looking at any access you have to a down payment. This can be existing cash, existing stocks, equity in your home, or even equity in grandparents' homes. The priority is to buy a good rental property that has the ability to grow for another fifteen to twenty years. Your down payment might be $50K-$100K now, but it will be significantly less expensive than trying to gift $1M down payment in twenty years in cash. You might not have $50K-$100K in cash, but you might have access to this down payment in the form of an LOC. If you serviced a $50K LOC at 6%, this is only $250/m. A $50K down payment can get you a $250K two-bed condo. By the time the child needs a home, you can sell the property and use the equity as their down payment. The hard part will be finding this investment property with a low vacancy rate and good rental potential in a growing area. This is why a DIP advisor is needed.

Chapter 12: Setting Up the Next Generation

Why do we work so hard? So we can create a better life for ourselves and our children. How can we best pass on wealth to the next generation? First, we can instill habits of discipline and of delaying gratification. Second, we can expose them to financial wealth formulas such as the DIP strategy, emphasizing the importance of investment real estate. Third, we can set them up with the equity in our real estate assets while living, and ensure a good estate plan for the passing of these assets when we die. The average Canadian will not give their children their RRSPs while living, which is why RRSPs will not create generational wealth. Conversely, our investment real estate can be used to fund our retirement as well as setting up the next generation to start building their wealth.

Envision how much further you would be financially if your first down payment had been gifted to you in your twenties. Or, if upon marrying you had been given a home, fully paid for. Both of these scenarios did occur for my uncle to his children. For my family, my wife and I own enough real estate now so that when our daughters are in their twenties, we will be able to fund their down payments or pay for a smaller place outright. Either way, our girls will have a leg up, which will let them focus on their careers and their families with less financial stress than many of their peers.

How can you help your children financially without jeopardizing your own retirement savings? With RRSPs/ TFSAs, you typically cannot but when you own investment real estate, you can. You have three options. First, you can sell the property, take the equity, and give what your kids need for their down payment. Whatever is left over, you can invest into a conservative stock portfolio and live off that. However, you will be taxed for capital gains, and the property is no longer growing in value. Therefore, this is our least favoured option.

The second option: you could live off the cash flow of the rent, and take a HELOC against the property and gift it to your kids. This will allow the property to keep growing. If you do not want to diminish your cash flow, you can let your adult child service the interest on the HELOC. This is a fair trade for providing them with the down payment. When you eventually sell the property or die, you can let the equity of the property pay out the leveraged funds.

The third option is that you can HELOC the down payment for your children, but also utilize the HELOC for your retirement. Any money used from the HELOC will be tax-free, but more importantly, it will allow for the property to keep growing. You are now drawing on as much HELOC tax-free as possible, thereby preserving the asset's ability to keep growing. If you plan on never selling the property, then it will be considered disposed of at the death of you or your spouse, whichever is last. This taxable disposition can be minimized with a good insurance estate planning strategy to take care of any outstanding loans and taxes. See Appendix 4: Why You Need Insurance as an Asset Class.

You might argue that if your real estate strategy in retirement is simply leveraging equity out to spend, while allowing the original asset to grow, then why not do that with RRSPs or other stock investments? People do not leverage against their stocks because of dangers of such things as a margin call. How many advisors would encourage this in retirement? Probably none. The point I am making is that when you have investment real estate in retirement, you have multiple options. When you only have stocks, you do not. If I sell my stocks in retirement, then I am taxed on that. If I leverage against my real estate investments, there is no taxation on it. Yes, there is interest accumulating, but we still have the asset increasing and rental cash flowing. As well, upon death, the asset itself could pay out the interest if you decided to only service the minimum. This is a tax-efficient advantage of freeing up cash.

> **Using the DIP strategy, what is the ideal property to buy if I am starting a family?**
>
> The ideal property is a single-family house with a rental suite that can also be rented through Airbnb. Remember, in the first stage of wealth building you are trying to increase income, reduce expenses, and invest in cash-flowing assets. A standard house with no suite will have none of these attributes. A house with a suite will have the ability to generate rental income, and CRA will allow you to deduct portions of the mortgage, property tax, heating, upgrades, etc. This will reduce your housing expenses. If the entire home is in a desirable Airbnb area, then the cost can be offset by renting out the home on Airbnb, thereby being cash-flow neutral or even positive while you vacation.
>
> The savings from these Airbnb-funded vacations can then go to buying more investment properties. For example, you buy a house with three bedrooms up and one bedroom down that can be used as a rental suite. The three bedrooms up you use for yourself and your children while they are young. You rent out the suite until the kids need more room. At that time, without having to move, you

can take back the rental suite for yourself, as opposed to upgrading your home. This will save you the transaction costs of realtor fees and property transfer tax, as well as the hassle of moving. You can still generate cash flow from the home when you take those wonderful vacations because the home is Airbnb-possible. When you sell the home, all of the equity will be capital gains tax-free because, since the date of purchase, it was your primary residence.

How can I use my personal property to help my children with their own property?

If you can afford a house with a larger yard, then see the zoning rules on laneway homes, often called coach homes. If your home will allow it, you have options down the road. For example, buying a house with a rental suite that also generates income from Airbnb or long-term rental will eventually result in taxable income. You want to continue to grow your assets, while minimizing taxation. Your home should have equity after a few years that can be borrowed against using a HELOC.

Consider building a coach home with the equity on the HELOC. The cash flow from the rental can be used to service the HELOC interest. Once the coach home is built you have another revenue generating source, but because of the high expense to build it there will be several years of deductions, keeping your taxation down. When it comes time to sell your home, you have now added value while reducing your taxes in using the equity to finance the coach home.

If you live in a very expensive area such as Metro Vancouver or the GTA, your adult children may have trouble buying back into the neighbourhood in which they grew up. This new coach home gives you the option to have one of your adult children move in, thereby keeping them close, and you close to your grandchildren. This strategy will have added a few hundred thousand to the sale of your home.

Furthermore, you should see if the property you are buying is zoned to allow it to be divided into a double lot in the future. If that is not the case when you buy, try to get an understanding of whether densification rules will likely cause the zoning laws to change in the future. If your property can be split into two, then you will have the ability to add more value to the property by rezoning your lot in the future.

Further, if you want to give a leg up to your kids, you can give one of the lots to the first one to marry. They finance the building of a new home. I have recommended this strategy for a client who had an adult child who was getting married. The couple could only afford a small two-bed condo in Vancouver. However, they could afford to build on the parents' property for the same cost as the two-bedroom condo. The result: a 2400 square foot home, as opposed to a 700 square foot two-bedroom condo.

A rule in real estate to remember: when you have a house with land, you have more options for you, your family, and the next generation.

Chapter 13: How You Are Underutilizing Your Realtor and Mortgage Broker

Most people have used a realtor and mortgage broker when buying their home. As well, many have a financial advisor and an accountant whom they meet with yearly. But, very few integrate all of them as their financial team to growth wealth. This entails meeting with all of them regularly, discussing financial goals, and implementing a strategy, and most importantly, having them communicate with each other. Conversely, wealthy investors have teams such as these, counselling them, bringing them new ideas, new investments, and collaborating on a strategy to incorporate their next investment.

A good starting point is your mortgage broker. This person will be the key in knowing how much you qualify for at any given time. More importantly, they can be creative in letting you know the strategies available for investing in your next rental property. When it came time to renew my personal mortgage years ago, Dara, a mortgage broker I had never used before, did a comparison with the bank I was currently with. He compared the options he had with his carriers, and concluded that I was better off staying with my own bank, even though some of his carriers had lower rates. I was confused why he would not want my new business. He explained that the conditions to break were not favourable, and if I stayed variable and overfunded the monthly payments, I'd actually be further ahead in the long run. When I did the calculations myself, I realized he was correct. He earned no commission that year, but he gained my trust. On my next transaction, he did an amazing job in strategizing the use of HELOCs, saving me over $10K in bridge financing. I work with various mortgage brokers who specialize with commercial, residential, multi-unit, and out of country properties.

Green Team Mortgages has done an outstanding job for real estate investors across Canada. I like Kyle and his team for three main reasons. First, they focus on investors looking to purchase not only locally but across Canada. Second, they can assist in investments that include residential and commercial real estate transactions. Finally, they have an outstanding educational format online where they teach Canadian investors how not to make mistakes, and how to take advantage of the real estate environment as it changes. An outstanding mortgage broker on your financial team can mean the difference between you owning one property or ten in your lifetime.

We tend to underutilize our realtors and mortgage brokers because we do not associate them with someone who can enhance our wealth. Instead, we keep their role limited to being the person we call when we want to buy or sell our own home. If you want to break your wealth ceiling, then this is a big mistake. If a friend mentioned that his advisor helped him to receive a double-digit annual return on his investments over the past ten years, which was paying a cash-flowing monthly dividend, you would likely want to speak with them immediately. However, would you be surprised to find out that it is your friend's realtor whom she is referring to?

A good realtor is like a good doctor. They are giving you advice with your best interest in mind. There are some commission-driven realtors that have their best interest at heart. They are the ones you want to avoid. I have been fortunate enough to have worked with many great realtors in my life. Years ago, I wanted to sell a Vancouver property when the market was cooling. I needed the capital to qualify to buy my own house in a few years. Realtor Marty did a full analysis of the market and my current situation, and heavily encouraged me to not sell that year. He knew the reason I was trying to sell, and the price I was hoping to get. He did not know how long it would take the market to recover, but he felt confident it would be within the next two years. He made no money by encouraging me not to sell, but he definitely earned my respect. Nine months later, he reached out to me, letting me know that conditions were now favourable for me to get the price I was hoping for. We listed, and even received a few thousand dollars more than I hoped for. A side note: he was not the realtor I used to buy the property, but was the seller's realtor for my first purchase several years prior. I was so impressed by his professionalism and his understanding of the property and the market that I promised myself that when it was time to sell the condo, I would reconnect with him to represent me. I estimate that Marty made me another $40K by having me not sell nine months earlier. This was over twenty years ago, and he was the first investment realtor I built a relationship with.

More recently, I have used realtor Ryan several times. You might be wondering why I did not use Marty. I highly recommend that you use investment-focussed realtors that specialize in certain areas. At the time, Ryan focussed on a different area in Metro Vancouver that I showed interest in. However, I did not know a lot about the area. He showed me the areas that he thought had great potential. Finding cash-flowing properties was the next big challenge, which is often the case for investors. However, because Ryan was used to working with investment-focussed realtors, we were able to find a two-bed condo that was eligible for being a corporate mid-term rental. These are rentals that are meant for one-to-six months usage only. They are often rented through a rental agency providing monthly rentals for insurance claims, or corporate executives that need a place to stay for a few months.

If I rented the condo as a long-term yearly rental, I would have yielded approximately $1200/m at the time of purchase. Instead, as a mid-term corporate rental I was netting between $1800-$2300/m on average. This was taking into account 40% property management fees, and the cost to furnish the property. A novice investor would hear "40% management fees" and likely would not move forward with the investment. But I collaborated with this investment-focussed realtor and with the mortgage broker, and I acted as the financial advisor. We were able to determine that the property was a sound investment. At time of purchase seven years ago, the property was bought at $250K. Today it is valued at $550K. Since day 1, I have been receiving approximately 30-40% above-market monthly long-term rental rates, which equates to $500-$1000/m more in rental income. Coincidently, the down payment was about equivalent to the extra amount that Marty had made me by encouraging me not to sell in the down year. If I do not sell the two-bed condo, it should be worth $1.1M by the time I retire. Without my investment realtors being a part of my financial team, I could not have uncovered these opportunities on my own.

Recently, I have collaborated with an amazing investment real estate team in BC known as Amy & Ally. I really love how they educate people, especially young women, encouraging them to invest as early as possible.

As a financial advisor, I recommend the integration of rental real estate for all my clients looking to grow beyond their wealth ceiling. You can easily do this by including an experienced investment-focussed realtor and a mortgage broker on your financial team. I remind my clients that I do not get compensation if they purchase real estate through their realtors and mortgage brokers. You should not be buying one property every ten years; you should be buying one property every three years. If there is a great opportunity, you could be buying three properties in one year. Further, you need to be using both realtors and mortgage brokers to strategize how you will help your kids buy homes in ten years using the properties they are helping you to invest with now. These professionals should be working in conjunction with your DIP advisor to see if their properties can act as retirement vehicles, which in most cases they can.

Today, I work with realtors throughout B.C., Alberta, Ontario, the Maritimes, as well as the US and Mexico. I own condos, houses, and multi-units. I have long-term rentals, corporate rentals, and Airbnb properties. Without my relationships with the realtors, who are all looking out for my best interests, none of this could have been possible. Do they make a commission by selling a property? Of course they do. Might this bias them? Possibly. But this is why it is important that they are not the only person guiding your decision. A DIP advisor should be there to ensure a property fits with your overall strategy. The mortgage broker will be there to see what you qualify for, find you the best lender, and come up with creative strategies to fund the property. The realtor's job is to find you properties that are good investments. Then, the DIP advisor working with them both will be the key to ensuring you do not make any impulsive mistakes. Do not underutilize the three best players on your team.

Chapter 14: Traditional Financial Advisors Versus DIP Advisors

I have read many financial planning books, and I know many financial advisors. In general, they are all professional individuals who have their clients' best interest in mind. However, I have noticed that they are all biased in their recommendations. They may prefer cryptocurrency exposure, REITs, US stock ETFs, or individual stocks. If they are employed by a major bank, they are biased towards the basket of mutual funds that the company provides. When asked about buying a home, some like home ownership while others do not. I find younger popular advisors who have recently written bestsellers are encouraging people to rent. This can be very confusing and dangerous information. Similar to when our relatives or friends give us financial advice, they are well intentioned, but biased, and in most cases have no analytical foundation.

In our practice, we try hard not to fall into this trap. Remember, the trend is your friend. This is why we let the analysis guide our recommendations. As we like to say, the math never lies. A cost-benefit analysis helps to compare one outcome to another. For example, consider buying a home five years ahead of schedule and sacrificing the paying down of student loans and not contributing to your RRSPs. Is this a good decision? The answer is maybe. But, if you posed this question to ten different financial advisors, how many of them would encourage that you contribute nothing toward your RRSPs and instead use all of your assets for buying a home?

How many would answer the question on the spot without doing any analysis? How many could actually calculate how much further ahead you would be if you were to buy a home, or conversely, if you were to rent and prioritize paying down your loans and maxing out your RRSPs?

There is no clear answer, which is why we need a deeper form of mathematical analysis to help guide a financial decision. Many advisors use basic financial planning software to generate financial plans for clients, which is fine when your planning is basic. However, for people wanting a higher level of returns, a greater level of analysis is needed which no one software program can provide. A non-biased fee-for-service advisor, with a strong analytical background and experience, will help to guide you towards the best decision.

The many questions you want answered are now subject to the opinions of whoever you happen to be dealing with, whether they're in their twenties or their sixties. The more confident they look and talk, the more likely people will accept their opinion. I know people here in Vancouver who wanted to buy a home over the last ten to fifteen years, but their advisor did not create any type of road map for this to occur. In some instances, they encouraged people to come up with a larger down payment through their RRSP/TFSA contributions. Others were advised to wait until the real estate market went down to a point where they could afford it. Some individuals in Vancouver were thinking of buying investment property in B.C. over ten years ago, but were encouraged not to withdraw any money from their stock portfolio because "the real estate would not be a good investment."

For these people, inaction has led to a lost opportunity cost of between $400K and $1.2M in tax-free equity in the home they never bought but had the opportunity to buy over a decade ago.

In our practice, we work to create financial models unique to clients to decide which scenario is in their best interest. Most inputs, such as market returns or real estate growth rates, fluctuate, so our Monte Carlo analysis is used to break options down to probabilities of success. Clients have the right to know about alternative financial options, not just solutions involving traditional financial products.

Should my realtor and financial advisor be working together?

Yes. If you believe in building wealth through real estate, then they should be as important as your accountant, lawyer, and financial advisor. The majority of realtors I have worked with have been outstanding professionals. Their role is invaluable to their area of expertise, which is why they should be working as part of your financial team. A realtor will highlight why a potential property is a good investment, but they will likely not be doing any retirement planning for you. That's why you want to ensure you are working with the right financial advisor. The realtor plays a vital role, but should not be the sole person helping with your next investment. However, you will not want an advisor who only believes in building wealth through the stock market if you do not share that vision. It will be frustrating for your realtor, and confusing for you not knowing who to listen to. If the purchase will affect your overall financial situation, then your financial advisor should be involved in the process. However, it should be an advisor who is philosophically aligned and actively supports your goals to create wealth with properties, and not an advisor who has an opposing view on wealth creation.

Once you are working with an advisor who has the same philosophy of building wealth through real estate, it is important they have the capability to analyze your options presented by your trusted realtors. For example, an investor owns real estate, and would like to buy more. They are looking in two areas, Vancouver and Calgary, and have partnered with different trusted realtors in each area. Both realtors are showing great investment rentals. In Vancouver the one-bedroom condo once listed for $650,000 now has a motivated seller listing at $599,000. It generates $1800 per month in rent with a $400/m condo fee. The Calgary realtor finds a house with two suites for $599,000, generating approximately $2400/m in rent. Which is the better investment? Vancouver with its historic high capital appreciation and low vacancy? Or the Calgary property having actual land, but a history of low capital appreciation. A fee-for-service DIP advisor who specializes in real estate will be non-biased in analyzing the Vancouver property compared to the Calgary one. This advisor will calculate, for each property, the cap rate, cash flow, and IRR to help guide the decision. Further, an outstanding DIP advisor will also compare those properties with in and out of province properties, and even some out of country. This is an incredible value added for serious investors wanting non-biased investment comparisons.

How important is it that my mortgage broker work with my financial advisor?

Incredibly important. Without them, you cannot qualify for the property you are trying to buy. They are critical in getting you the best rate for your investment. But not all mortgage brokers are created equal. How long have they been in the business? Can they qualify you for a commercial, or just a residential property? Are they associated with more than just A-lenders? The best mortgage brokers will not only qualify you for the property you are trying to buy, but they can also be instrumental in problem-solving solutions when you do not qualify. Some have an "it can't be done" attitude, while the good ones say "here's how it can be done." They might explore monetary gifts from family, using equity from another property, or liquidating another asset. However, this further strengthens your need for the DIP advisor's involvement to ensure that the financing of this purchase does not negatively affect your overall long-term financial situation. For example, for your own home, you can liquidate your RRSPs to buy a first home in Canada, but you need to pay back the RRSPs within fifteen years. The DIP advisor will ensure that you are in a position to do so.

You advisor needs to look carefully at how all your financial decisions affect your retirement. If you have no other source of retirement investments, such as a pension, then you might be endangering your ability to retire. For investment properties, you might already have a rental property that you are considering selling in order to help qualify to buy the new larger property. If should be the DIP advisor's role to analyze the impact of selling the original investment rental on your future finances. It could be a big mistake to do so. For example, imagine you were trying to buy a $2,000,000 multi-unit rental property, and you currently owned an $800,000 Vancouver rental condo that only had $200,000 remaining debt period. Being an avid real estate investor, you might want to sell the condo property to buy the larger multi-unit. However, this possibly is not the best financial option. The trusted mortgage broker will do her job by helping you to finance the purchase. But it is not her role to do any analysis on your long-term financial future, which is why a financial advisor needs to be involved. A DIP advisor specializing with real estate investors will be able to analyze the following options for you.

1. Sell the condo and buy the multi-unit.
2. Keep the condo and buy the multi-unit by selling other investments.
3. Buy the multi-unit by leveraging against the condo, thereby keeping both assets.
4. Keep the condo, and buy a different real estate investment altogether with better cap rates and cash flow.

A DIP advisor can do a cost-benefit analysis for all of these options determining which will yield the highest cash flow and future asset value in retirement. For the avid real estate investor, the high-functioning partnership between the realtor, mortgage broker, and financial advisor is essential. Getting this decision right could literally mean the difference of millions of dollars for your future.

Should I Use a Financial Advisor?

Do we actually need financial advisors? Today it is becoming more popular to not use financial advisors. We are getting more educated about advisors' fees in the form of high MERs and we want to avoid them.

People who are using financial advisors typically fall into one of three categories. First, there are people who do not know any better. Perhaps their parents have always used an advisor and now they are using an advisor. Or, they have walked into the bank, and that really friendly bank teller has flagged them as a financial investment client. They set up a meeting with a financial advisor, and once they start this relationship, it becomes hard to break. The second type of person uses an advisor because they want a method to invest that is easy and simple. They are not interested in becoming more financially savvy. They understand that there is a fee system, but want nothing to do with managing and investing their own portfolio.

The third category is the type of person who is a more sophisticated investor. He will listen to the blog posts and stay up to date on the markets. He will use an advisor, not due to apathy, but because he understands that someone else can provide more value than he can on his own. For him, the value outweighs the fees incurred. This last category of investor is why most people should use a financial advisor. You should always pay for a service where the value of the service outweighs the fees.

But, should you pay an advisor who cannot consistently beat the S&P 500 index? Probably not. If you could grow your wealth to $1M in retirement on your own, while saving $150K in fees, then why would you pay an advisor? However, if an advisor could grow your wealth to $5M, which you also realize that you cannot do on your own, would you pay $150K over a lifetime in fees? The answer should be "Yes." Once you realize that someone can provide more value than the cost of the service, and you also are honest in understanding that you cannot do this yourself, then yes, you should be paying someone to do this for you.

So, should you personally be using a financial advisor? The answer is, "It depends." What is your philosophy for growing wealth? If you do not have a philosophy on investing, then you should explore what multiple advisors do and see which strategy resonates with you. Some advisors' goal is to ensure that you are on track for retirement, while buying a home, and providing education for your kids. Great, if those are your only financial goals. Most families do need a financial advisor, much like they need a family dentist.

However, much like you would do with any professional service provider, you should leave them if you feel there is a better alternative elsewhere. If you are a DIY investor, and solely investing in stocks, then you definitely should explore a DIP advisor. Your opportunity cost to accelerate wealth is being lost each year. Remember, real estate is a long game; you need to take advantage of time. If you are a DIY investor that already invests in real estate, scaling to the larger deals such as multi-units, commercial, or joint venture might be how you take your wealth to the next level.

At Latitude West, our goals are for clients to live an abundant life in retirement and to have created generational wealth. We realize that traditional mutual funds and stocks and bonds will likely not get you there, so we include investment real estate recommendations. What is the key difference between our practice and that of a traditional financial advisor? Essentially it is in how we reach your end goals for your finances. The traditional advisor will be growing your wealth using the stock market as their primary focus, and we will be focussing on growth through real estate. Historically, the DIP strategy has grown assets beyond people's wealth ceiling by simply using real estate. You just need to follow the math.

Chapter 15: The Big Finish

"Life shrinks or expands in proportion to one's courage." *Anais Nin*

Jim Rohn, the famous motivational speaker, has said that there are two types of suffering in life when investing. The suffering of discipline, and the suffering of regret. The discipline is in saving when we would rather spend, when starting early rather than delaying. The regret is in not having enough in retirement, not being able to help our kids with any financial assistance, not taking advantage of an investment that we knew would lead to financial freedom. We are fortunate enough to live in a great country. We have the right to be educated enough to know how an ordinary person can have access to extraordinary wealth. I hope the ideas of this book have helped to broaden your mind as to what you can accomplish in your lifetime. I hope that it will give you the courage to step outside of your comfort zone moving forward with your finances.

My research has shown that the traditional investing that most Canadians are doing is not the formula that is going to create generational wealth. Using primarily a balanced stock portfolio, you will be lucky if it sustains you for your retirement years. I have been invested in both my RRSPs and in real estate for decades. Comparing the rates of return of each investment side by side, the real estate overwhelmingly beats out my stock portfolio. Will the average Canadian be able to accumulate wealth in the multi-millions by retirement through their stock portfolio? None that I have seen. Conversely, I am part of Canadian real estate network groups with average Canadians as members. I have met Uber drivers, teachers, nurses, and self-employed small business owners that all own rental properties, and some with as many as thirty properties. These are average Canadians with average jobs, and they are all breaking their average wealth ceilings with real estate. This is my goal for you as well.

Will you create a life for yourself and your family with no regrets? The purpose of this book is not to get you to invest in real estate nor to change any of the things that you are doing currently that are working. The purpose of the book is to educate you as to what your options are in order to have a greater financial life beyond your wealth ceiling. The strategies and ideas may not resonate with everyone, nor should they. There is additional work involved with this type of investing, which includes an expanding of your risk tolerance, and time dedicated towards your investments. However, I have found, and many of my clients have also found, that this road is worth taking.

Today (2024) the richest person in the world is Elon Musk with a $242B net worth. However, Andrew Carnegie (1900), the founder of US Steel, was worth $310B if his wealth was adjusted to today's dollars, making him wealthier than Elon Musk if they were to be compared today. Carnegie gave away most of his wealth before he passed away as well as much wisdom for young people trying to gain wealth. One of his is most famous quotes is:

"Ninety percent of all millionaires become so through owning real estate. More money has been made in real estate than in all industrial investments combined. The wise young man or wage earner of today invests his money in real estate."
Carnegie's advice is over one hundred years old, but continues to ring true today.

At the beginning of this book, I asked, "Who is the greatest person you know?" I believe that if you shift your mind to a better way of investing, you will live the life of abundance, generosity, and financial freedom that we all deserve. And, at the end of your life, the greatest person you will know... will be you. God Bless.

Appendix I

The Problem with Modern Portfolio Theory

In 1611, the first stock market was created in Amsterdam. In 1952, Harry Markowitz developed the Modern Portfolio Theory (MPT). This was the birth of today's diversification of securities in order to correlate an individual's return with their risk.

More recently, the Lindy Effect was mathematically explained by economist/mathematician Nassim Nicholas Taleb. It theorizes that the longer a period that something has existed, the longer its life expectancy. For example, the longer a show has lasted on Broadway, the longer it is predicted to stay on Broadway. The formula that Taleb uses to calculate the longevity of a new phenomenon, such as MPT, is illustrated below.

$$E[T - t | T > t] = pxt$$

Modern Portfolio Theory has been around for approximately seventy years and its authority is widely accepted, but it has one great limitation for people trying to break their wealth ceiling. The people it was intended to help are not getting rich. If you disagree, find me a list of middle class income earners who have used MPT and have become rich.

However, the asset allocation of the Talmud has been around for over 3000 years. With a basic understanding of the Lindy Effect, we can be confident that the Talmud teachings for becoming wealthy will likely be around for another thousand years. Can we say the same for MPT? How many people have broken their occupations' wealth ceiling using MPT? Alternatively, do you know any middle class income earners who have invested a portion of their income in real estate and have become rich? I know more than I can count. Just go to any real estate networking group and ask the same question. Are you using MPT to grow your wealth? If you knew that a better method existed, would you try it?

Appendix 2

Kids' Education: RESP Versus Real Estate

How are you saving for your child's education?

When my first daughter, Isabella, was born, I owned two rental properties and my own townhouse. My wife wanted us to set up an RESP, as most Canadians were encouraged to do, through the Canada Education Savings Grant (CESG). The government gives a maximum of $500/year towards the RESP if you contributed $2500 annually. It sounded like a no-brainer, and seemed to be the responsible thing to do.

Three years later, my second daughter was born, and I was just finishing my MBA. I felt that starting the second RESP for Maddie was also the logical thing to do. Luckily, my MBA experience had equipped me with the ability to do a cost-benefit analysis. As a real estate investor, I was always looking for my next investment, so I decided to compare the amount I would put towards Isabella's and Maddie's RESP versus buying another property. I had found a property in the Fraser Valley, a $340K Abbotsford house in a good middle class neighbourhood that I was considering buying. The down payment and interest rates at the time would cause a cash flow breakeven.

However, if I used the HELOC out of one of my existing properties to purchase this property, it would generate somewhere between $200-$300 of negative cash flow per month, depending on the vacancy rate, interest rates, and capital expenditures. I decided to do both: invest in the home with the HELOC and invest in the girls' RESPs. I used a family RESP plan, so I was actually just adding onto Isabella's RESP. I have contributed approximately $600/m since 2010, when my third daughter, Olivia, was born.

What was the result of the comparison? The total value of my RESP family plan is approximately $110,000 by the time Isabella was eighteen years old, and that includes the government's portion. In comparison, the Abbotsford house that I bought with the HELOC minus the property tax, minus the realtor fees that would be needed if I sold the property, as well as paying out the capital gains tax, would net approximately $680,000 net profit. The real estate investment was the winner by an outrageous landslide.

If you are thinking that I just got lucky on the house, you would be wrong. I knew that houses grew in value around 5-6% in the Lower Mainland area. Based on my analysis and research, I believed we would have an increase in migration east, out into the Fraser Valley, due to the affordability and low housing inventory levels in Vancouver. All came true.

The house I found was in a popular school catchment neighbourhood that was undervalued due to the $20,000 of repairs needed, which I did over the course of three years. But I'll be clear: the property I bought needed to fit specific criteria with regards to vacancy rate, down payment, growth rate, cap rate, and the type of home itself.

If you could find a property that would also be able to pay the HELOC's monthly interest, then you definitely have found a golden gem. If you do not, then you could use the amount that would otherwise be contributed to the RESP towards the servicing of the HELOC.

Now, a couple of things that made a big difference with the

Abbotsford house versus the RESP. First, the house needed work done in year one, then again another five times over the next fifteen years. I did none of the work myself, rather I hired contractors to do it for me. I did need to find them and supervise the work, as well as making any major decisions. However, this was not new to me since I was already an investor. At last count, I have spent close to $50,000 over the fifteen years. But each time I needed a capital expenditure, I just used the HELOC to pay for it, and I deducted the interest each year.

Second, each year the market rate of the rent kept going up and the mortgage kept going down. By the sixth year, the property rent had gone up enough to fully cover all the expenses including the HELOC. So this gave an unfair major advantage to the property over the RESP. This advantage meant I did not have to keep contributing each year in order to maintain or grow the real estate investment. I actually did not add any extra cash from my personal funds unlike the regular RESP contributions needed.

Finally, and probably most significant, because the equity value of the property was so substantial, I was able take another HELOC against the property in 2014, and buy a two-bed Abbotsford condo for $250K. It was a home run investment since the rent fully covered both the mortgage and the HELOC. The regular rental market was not able to achieve this, but I analyzed alternatives and found that a corporate rental property management company was able to achieve a cash-flowing revenue from the property. To date, the Abbotsford condo is worth $500,000, which was approximately a 10.4%/a rate of growth. The Abbotsford house is worth $1M, with two suites generating a net cash flow of $1600/m (or $19,200/a). This means that after I pay out the mortgage, taxes, and property management fees, I net $1600 per month. Further, the house generates enough annual cash flow to pay for Isabella's tuition and expenses for her post-secondary. So, I do not need to use her RESPs this coming year, and will likely just save it for my other two daughters.

Should you be doing this for your children? The answer is maybe. What is your comfort level? What is your knowledge base? Can you find this place on your own? Do you incorporate an advisor who's able to do this?

Am I telling people to buy real estate instead of RESPs? Maybe. Are you OK with the extra work involved with buying real estate? Yes? Then, are you able to find a property that fits similar criteria? If not, but you still want to do this, then you need the right financial advisor who specializes in this real estate strategy.

If my daughters have their own children, I will not be encouraging them to invest in their kids' RESPs. I will instead help them to invest in a property that will grow over eighteen years and produce cash flow. I am confident they will receive a similar outstanding result.

Appendix 3

Real Estate Versus Loans: Which Should You Prioritize?

I have serviced young graduating doctors and dentists as clients for many years now. The cost of their tuition has grown exponentially from when I first started working with these groups. For example, a dentist in Canada on student loans can expect to finish school with around $350K of debt, not including their undergraduate loans. If they received their education internationally, such as the US, then this number can be even higher. Once they graduate, they will have sacrificed a minimum of eight years to their post-secondary education. These young medical professionals will now be eager to start building wealth. But they will be faced with a new problem: Where do they prioritize their first financial goal? Their three main options: pay off loans, invest in the stock market, or buy real estate.

Most of these young doctors I have worked with tend to prioritize their student loans. This is for two reasons. First, it is the easier decision since no real work or research is needed to implement this strategy. They just simply pay as much as possible towards their debt until it is paid off. Second, many new grads are uncomfortable with holding large amounts of debt once they have finished and are working. They feel they will sleep better at night knowing that their loans are fully paid off. I completely understand this since I had four university degrees to pay down on my own when I was younger. However, this is a different world we now live in with the high cost of housing. Advice from the last generation might not apply to those now starting out on their financial journey.

When I work with clients, I try not to tell them what to do. Instead, my role is to analyze each of their options. This will allow them to make the best decision based on the informed data I have gathered. For example, let's take Dr. Jane Smith, a newly graduated dentist wanting to buy a home, pay down loans, and save for retirement. Although she is my client, I will not tell her what to do. Instead, I will conduct a cost-benefit analysis on all three options she is considering prioritizing.

First, we analyze the loans. After tax, she will be making between $120K to $180K depending on how skilled she is, and the how busy the practice. If she lives modestly, she can aggressively pay down her loans contributing $60K annually, which is between a third and half of the average first year dentist's income. To note, this is a large sacrifice. If living in an expensive area, such at Metro Vancouver or the GTA, there will not be much extra income for extravagant vacations or cars, let alone to save for a down payment. The strategy of loan repayment will pay down loans quickly, but at the requirement of living frugally. If Dr. Smith graduated at age twenty-six, and was to pay $60K annually toward her $350K loans, it would take her 7.7 years to pay back the loans fully. This would put her at age thirty-three when finished. But her net worth would still be at zero since she did not buy a home or invest in the stock market. So her loans would be finished, but she would still have to save for a down payment and invest for retirement. Is this the best financial strategy?

If we look to investing in the stock market instead, we now need an investment that will compete with the 6.95% annual rate of return that the loans were charging. As well, this investment would be a guaranteed 6.95% after-tax return. Nonetheless, whether you use a TFSA, an RRSP, or a non-registered investment, we can all agree that the return would need to be higher than 6.95%. To note, from 2000 to today (2023), the S&P 500 has returned 6.93% annually. If you adjust for inflation, it is 4.34%. However, paying down loans is a guaranteed investment with almost zero standard deviation. The S&P 500 has averaged a 16% standard deviation in its returns. There is nothing wrong with investing in the stock market, but investors with high debts should understand the cost-benefit of doing so.

S&P 500 Stocks

Finally, let us consider buying real estate over paying down $350K of loans. If you live in an area that has a history of expensive real estate, then I highly recommend this type of analysis be conducted. In Metro Vancouver, a condo will average around $800K. If this is your principal residence, then a 5% down payment ($40K) is the minimum required by the bank to approve your loan. You will have a CMHC insurance fee to pay for mortgages less than 20% down payment, but this can be included into your mortgage. Statistically, Vancouver home prices have appreciated at 8.5% over the last twenty years. Will this rate continue? According to the Globe and Mail, a

2022 study showed that Canada will need another 3.5M more housing units by 2030 in order to bring our housing back to a balanced market. Unfortunately, this would require us to triple our current housing production in a system that is already at full capacity, which according to the article, is impossible. What does this imply? There will be a high demand, with a lack of supply for housing, therefore housing prices in Canada should continue to increase at the current rate, or go even higher.

Vancouver Housing Markets

Canada Housing Crisis

To get a full understanding of whether to pay back loans or to buy your first property, let me take an example of two dental students, Dr. Smith from the example above and Dr. Bill Jones, who both graduated in 2015. Both were aged twenty-six, and both graduated with $350K in loans that were all consolidated into an LOC. Both had the opportunity to buy a home in Vancouver for $500K in 2015. Dr. Smith chose not to buy the home, instead continue to rent, and aggressively pay back the loans. With the LOC interest rates averaging 2.6%, it has taken her 6.4 years to pay the loans back fully. By 2021 the loans were fully paid off. But her net assets were still at zero. For the home she wishes to own, she must start saving for a down payment. Unfortunately for her, Vancouver housing prices appreciated at an average of 9% over this time period. In one year, she saved aggressively and had enough for the down payment in 2022 on the same home she could have bought upon graduating. The $500K property from 2015 cost $946,891 in 2022. Dr. Smith aggressively paid back $350K of loans beginning at age twenty-six and by age thirty-three she bought the same place but for $496,891 more in purchase price. Comparatively, she is now further behind financially with this decision.

Dr. Jones, on the other hand, decided to buy his first property in 2015. He understood that a home is an appreciating asset, which is capital gains tax-free if it is a personal property in Canada. He serviced only the minimum of his LOC, which required approximately $10K for the year. He had the $25K (5%) down payment after a few months of working and purchased the property. The CMHC requires an insurance fee to be paid when paying less than 5% down payment for a property. For Dr. Jones's home, this was $19K, but it was added onto his overall mortgage, now totalling $494K. He had a lending rate of 2.7% at the time using a thirty-year amortization. By 2022, his mortgage balance was $487,712K with a property worth $946,891. The equity in the property is therefore worth $459,179. In 2016, after Dr. Jones bought his home and was no longer paying rent, he then started to aggressively pay down his loans. However, his home purchase required an extra $10K annually over the rent he would have paid, so he was now contributing only $50K annually from 2016 to 2022. In the same year that Dr. Smith paid off her loans fully, Dr. Jones still had an LOC balance of $88K.

However, he also owned a property worth $946,891, and had not been paying rent for the last seven years. The monthly cost of rent was instead going towards paying down equity in his own home. These two stories are not uncommon for young grads with high debts. Each may have had no regrets with their financial decisions, but today's professionals starting out do need to become more financially educated before deciding a financial path.

If you are living in an area that has housing costs rapidly increasing due to a lack of supply, you are likely better off buying as fast as possible. If you have the opportunity to live at home, then you should consider buying an investment property in the same area to rent out. You will enjoy the same capital appreciation and be able to deduct multiple items on your taxes such as mortgage interest, property management, strata, and insurance fees. However, this might not be as simple as it sounds because of the many changes to the environment. For example, the interest rates might go higher, the housing market might have slowed down, you might not know where you are planning on living in the next five years, and so on. This is why a DIP advisor is most valuable in times when you need a cost-benefit analysis performed before making your next financial decision.

Appendix 4

Why You Need Insurance as an Asset Class

Insurance has always been used to protect against risk. It is needed in case of an unfortunate event. Why do the wealthy use this as an asset class? Three main reasons for investors are tax, tax, tax. First, it is significantly more tax efficient at passing wealth to the next generation. Second, it can be more tax efficient in utilizing its equity value when compared to other investments, such as stocks or bonds. Lastly, if incorporated, you overfund a policy letting it grow tax free, borrow out the cash value tax free, deduct the interest for investments reducing your taxable income, receive a death benefit to pay out debts tax free, and receive a Capital Dividend Account (CDA) credit allowing assets to flow out of the corporation tax free. All investors are leaving money on the table without an insurance strategy combined with their investments.

For the majority of people, insurance can be confusing. Insurance brokers are mostly outstanding professionals, but they are compensated through commissions. As with any commission-based business, they are incentivized to sell the largest premium possible to potential clients. Unfortunately, this has caused many people to be skeptical of all insurance products. For low to middle income earners, buying term insurance and investing the difference between the cost of term and permanent insurance often does make the most sense. However, for individuals with substantial wealth to be passed to spouse and kids, permanent insurance often acts as an asset class with more tax efficiency than any stock, bond, or real estate can provide.

Once you are on the path to breaking your wealth ceiling, a proper insurance needs analysis can help to determine what the impending tax implication will be. Using a universal life or a whole life product will often be a better investment due to the tax-free payout upon death. Wealthy individuals know that they will not die penniless. In other words, they will be passing wealth on to the next generation. The question is: Would they rather give the government or their kids the greater piece of the pie?

Below is an example of a client, John Smith, with three current investment properties inside a holding corporation, and he intends on buying another for $2M approximately in five years. We have estimated the growth rate of each property in order to determine the capital gains tax in the future.

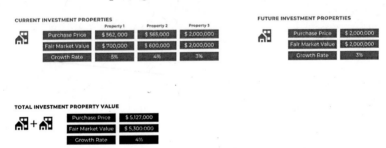

CURRENT INVESTMENT PROPERTIES

	Property 1	Property 2	Property 3
Purchase Price	$ 562, 000	$ 565,000	$ 2,000,000
Fair Market Value	$ 700,000	$ 600,000	$ 2,000,000
Growth Rate	5%	4%	3%

FUTURE INVESTMENT PROPERTIES

Purchase Price	$ 2,000,000
Fair Market Value	$ 2,000,000
Growth Rate	3%

TOTAL INVESTMENT PROPERTY VALUE

Purchase Price	$ 5,127,000
Fair Market Value	$ 5,300,000
Growth Rate	4%

With real estate you do not have to pay any capital gains on a property until it is sold or until you pass away. If we assume that he never sells the real estate, and passes away in fifty years, below we can see the expected tax bill awaiting his estate to be paid out. This is approximately $6M.

Year	Property 1	Property 2	Property 3	New Property 4	Capital Gains	Deferred Taxes Due
1	$700,000	$600,000	$2,000,000		$173,000	-$46,278
2	$735,000	$624,000	$2,060,000		$292,000	-$78,110
3	$771,750	$648,960	$2,121,800		$415,510	-$111,149
4	$810,338	$674,918	$2,185,454		$543,710	-$145,442
5	$850,854	$701,915	$2,251,018	$2,000,000	$676,787	-$181,041
10	$1,085,930	$853,987	$2,609,546	$2,318,548	$1,741,011	-$465,721
15	$1,385,952	$1,039,006	$3,025,179	$2,687,833	$3,010,970	-$805,435
20	$1,768,865	$1,264,110	$3,507,012	$3,115,935	$4,528,922	-$1,211,487
25	$2,257,570	$1,537,982	$4,065,588	$3,612,222	$6,346,363	-$1,697,652
30	$2,881,295	$1,871,191	$4,713,131	$4,187,556	$8,526,173	-$2,280,751
35	$3,677,344	$2,276,590	$5,463,811	$4,854,525	$11,145,269	-$2,981,359
40	$4,693,326	$2,769,820	$6,334,054	$5,627,725	$14,297,924	-$3,824,695
45	$5,990,005	$3,369,909	$7,342,905	$6,524,076	$18,099,894	-$4,841,722
50	$7,644,933	$4,100,010	$8,512,439	$7,563,192	$22,693,573	-$6,070,531
55	$9,757,087	$4,988,289	$9,868,250	$8,767,812	$28,254,438	-$7,558,062
60	$12,452,791	$6,069,016	$11,440,006	$10,164,297	$34,999,110	-$9,362,262

To pay for this pending tax bill, our client can start to do some financial planning with us to prepare. We have narrowed it down to three options:

1. Sell one or more properties.

   Pro: You do not have to deal with any planning until you pass away.

   Con: You will be taxed on the capital gain, and your asset will now cease to grow. If you were making monthly cash flow, this too would end. As well, you are subject to the conditions of the market. Real estate prices could be down, or low demand may cause vultures to low-ball desperate sellers. Or, you might not be able to sell at all if there are no buyers willing to buy.

2. Sell another asset, such as stocks.

   Pro: You can liquidate a stock more easily than selling a real estate property.

   Cons: Similar to option 1, you will be taxed on the capital gains, and the asset will cease to grow.

3. Incorporate an insurance solution.

   Pro: If you start early enough, it will be significantly less expensive than option 1 or 2. You will have accurate future values for the insurance investment because the volatility is much lower than on the stock or real estate market. The payout is tax free, and it will likely be a less expensive investment compared to investing in stocks. A permanent policy with cash value also enables you to leverage against the equity tax free to reinvest in other assets, such as more real estate.

   Con: You need to qualify for the insurance policy. You need to be comfortable with paying for the insurance, typically by shifting investment dollars from another asset.

A strategy that we often recommend for real estate investors is to use the cash flow of the property to fund the insurance policy. With all cash-flowing properties, you have two choices for what to do with the extra funds. First, you can spend them. There is, of course, no tax or investment advantage to this. Second, you can invest them. But, if you were to reinvest the money, what asset class would you put it in, and why?

Here are the corporate tax rates on investments in B.C.

PERSONAL TAXATION OF INVESTMENTS	
Interest income · Rent, GICs, bonds, etc.	Up to 53.53%
Dividend income · Paid out of the profits from a corporation	Up to 47.74%
Capital gains income · Real estate and other investments that is sold at a higher price than the purchase price	Up to 26.76%
Estate bond · Cash value growth and death benefit	As low as 0.00%

If the property is meant to be passed on to your children, then using a product such as an insurance estate bond would be recommended. An estate bond is similar to a regular bond because it will grow at a conservative rate of 4-6%. However, unlike a regular bond, it will also come with a death benefit that is paid out tax-free. The ROI on the death benefit is incredibly large in the early years if you were to pass away prematurely. If you were to pass away at life expectancy, then it still makes for a great stable investment. For John Smith, age forty-two, we determined that a whole life policy paid over only ten years would satisfy his tax issue. It would require a $50,500 annual investment using corporate dollars; over ten years this totals a $505,00 investment.

	INVESTMENT PROPERTY VALUES					ESTATE BOND VALUES		
Year	Property 1	Property 2	Property 3	New Property 4	Deferred Taxes Due	Premium	Death Benefit	Cash Value
1	$700,000	$600,000	$2,000,000		-$46,278	$50,500	$2,728,184	$42,045
2	$735,000	$624,000	$2,060,000		-$78,110	$50,500	$2,956,430	$89,344
3	$771,750	$648,960	$2,121,800		-$111,149	$50,500	$3,183,858	$140,761
4	$810,338	$674,918	$2,185,454		-$145,442	$50,500	$3,409,978	$195,221
5	$850,854	$701,915	$2,251,018	$2,000,000	-$181,041	$50,500	$3,635,769	$253,064
10	$1,085,930	$853,987	$2,609,546	$2,318,548	-$465,721	$50,500	$4,764,369	$600,265
15	$1,385,952	$1,039,006	$3,025,179	$2,687,833	-$805,435		$2,957,689	$792,030
20	$1,768,865	$1,264,110	$3,507,012	$3,115,935	-$1,211,487		$3,209,597	$1,048,370
25	$2,257,570	$1,537,982	$4,065,588	$3,612,222	-$1,697,652		$3,520,961	$1,388,206
30	$2,881,295	$1,871,191	$4,713,131	$4,187,556	-$2,280,751		$3,893,428	$1,831,518
35	$3,677,344	$2,276,590	$5,463,811	$4,854,525	-$2,981,359		$4,329,368	$2,397,563
40	$4,693,326	$2,769,820	$6,334,054	$5,627,725	-$3,824,695		$4,764,369	$3,108,258
45	$5,990,005	$3,369,909	$7,342,905	$6,524,076	-$4,841,722		$5,406,533	$3,968,641
50	$7,644,933	$4,100,010	$8,512,439	$7,563,192	-$6,070,531		$6,058,741	$4,907,348
55	$9,757,087	$4,988,289	$9,868,250	$8,767,812	-$7,558,062		$6,792,694	$5,974,835
60	$12,452,791	$6,069,016	$11,440,006	$10,164,297	-$9,362,262		$7,625,202	$6,932,015

Our client will want to know why this is a better strategy than investing in the stock market in order to achieve the same goal with the $50,500 annual investment over the ten years. Below is a direct comparison using a 7%/a return for an equity investment.

STOCK INVESTMENTS

Annual Deposit	$ 50,500
Deposit Period	10 Years
Rate of Return	7%
Investment Type	Public Stocks

ESTATE BOND

Annual Deposit	$ 50,500
Deposit Period	10 Years
Dividend Scale	Current
Investment Type	Smoothed Return

STOCK INVESTMENTS (Age 90)

Pre-Tax Value: $ 6,854,798

Net Estate Value: $ 4,197,909

Lost to Taxes: $ 2,656,889

ESTATE BOND (Age 90)

Total Insurance: $ 6,058,741

Net Estate Value: $ 6,058,741

Strategy Advantage: $ 1,860,831

The stock investment actually grosses more than the insurance in Year 50, but due to the 26.76% capital gains tax on stocks invested corporately, $2,656,889 is lost to taxation.

Conversely, the insurance strategy using the estate bond has no taxation thereby allowing the full $6,058,741 to be used for the capital gains tax bill. This strategy shows a $1,860,831 advantage over the stock. Further, stocks come with a much higher volatility for growth. The S&P 500 has a standard deviation of approximately 15%, while the dividend rate achieved for a permanent whole life policy has typically been under 2%.

SPDR S&P 500 (SPY) ETF

If you were incorporated and had assets in the corporation such as real estate, this strategy works even better because it will come with a Capital Dividend Account (CDA) credit. A CDA is a credit inside a corporation that passes assets tax-free out of the corporation to shareholders when sold. If you hold real estate assets inside a corporation you created, such as a holding company, you could have a very large capital gains tax when you sell or pass away. Some people are not fans of investing in life insurance because they never get to see the payout. However, an estate bond allows you to access the cash value during your lifetime. You can either take the cash surrender value, or you can take the cash by leveraging against the cash surrender value. For the latter, much like real estate, you can leverage the equity of an asset using a bank loan. For estate bonds, banks will lend 75-100% of the cash surrender value tax free, depending on how it is structured.

The wealthy will do this for two reasons. First, it allows

them to withdraw the money tax free. Unlike regular stocks or bonds, there is no guaranteed death benefit. Banks will be willing to lend cash on a policy that has a guaranteed death benefit because they know they will get their loan back. Second, if the policyholder reinvests the loan money, he can actually deduct the interest on his taxes, thereby lowering his taxable income, while increasing his investable assets.

With this example, holding the estate bond until death will allow the beneficiaries to receive the tax-free death benefit, which will be used to take care of any probate and capital gains tax that your assets have accumulated in your lifetime. This will allow your children to receive the real estate and stock assets without having to sell them. Further, if incorporated, it will allow the CDA credit to pass the insurance proceeds tax-free to the shareholders and/or estate. And, any unused CDA credits can also be used for the tax-free passing of any other sold assets (stocks/bonds/real estate) also to the estate and the shareholders (spouse/kids).

Interestingly, the largest policies placed by insurance companies on individuals are for people who do not need the insurance. They have more than enough money to cover all of their family's expenses and income replacement if they were to pass away. However, they do need the insurance to minimize taxation to preserve their assets. Being fee-for-service advisors, and building a trusted relationship with clients is why our practice has grown so quickly over the past decade. There is no obligation to buy insurance when we take on a new client. If there is a significant benefit to placing a policy, then we will simply show the analysis and let the client decide. We want all of our clients to not only break their wealth ceiling, but to get their kids the largest head start in life as well.

Appendix 5

Should I Invest in Stocks or Real Estate When Saving for Retirement?

"It is easier to compete in the Olympics than it is in the stock market." Ray Dalio

Most Canadians and Americans are taught to save for retirement using their RRSPs (or 401K) plan. If their work has a matching program, then this type of investing becomes even more of an incentive. However, a small group of people are not doing this at all, and instead are using real estate as an alternative to save for this retirement. As well, this real estate strategy that we provide for our investment clients cannot be done with RRSPs but will amplify their wealth in retirement beyond what a stock only portfolio can provide.

We saw how the five-to-one rule of real estate can help to get double-digit returns on investments with leveraged real estate. To compare how you will invest for retirement, let's start with the RRSP argument. Say a married couple, both twenty-five years old, is to start investing in their TFSAs with $1000/m combined until age thirty. At a 7.5% rate of return, they would have approximately $72,000. At age thirty, they stop the $1000/m investments and shift the money into their RRSPs until age sixty-five without contributing any more money into their investment. Using a sensitivity analysis with stock market return rates of 4%, 7%, or 10%, they would now have the future amounts below at age sixty-five.

Investment rate	Age 30	Age 65	Age 85
4% (Low)	$72,000	$284,118	$622,538
7% (Med)	$72,000	$768,713	$2,974,680
10% (High)	$72,000	$2,023,375	$13,612,258

Using the DIP strategy, at age thirty I would encourage my client to consider the opportunity cost of investing in rental real estate instead. I would highlight that it is a more active investment needing more hands-on effort, but it is worth it. If we use $72,000 from TFSAs as a down payment for a $360K property, we know the property will grow over time. Low, medium, and high growth rates are different for real estate properties versus stock returns. Average property values typically appreciate at lower rates. For our comparison we will be using the lower values of 3%, 5%, or 7% real estate growth rates for the sensitivity analysis. The chart below shows the property valued at age sixty-five (retirement) and age eighty-five (life expectancy).

Down Payment - Age 30	Purchase Price	Growth Rates	Age 65	Age 85
$72,000	$360,000	3% (Low)	$1,012.990	$1,829,573
$72,000	$360,000	5% (Med)	$1,985,765	$5,268,827
$72,000	$360,000	7% (High)	$3,843,569	$14,873,400

When comparing the numbers, the returns on the real estate investments beat the RRSPs investments in all low, medium, and high return environments.

You might be in awe of the 7% growth rate and feel it is unreasonable for me to use. As I remind you, do not rely on speculation or emotion when making an investment decision. The trend is your friend. Always follow the numbers and let the math guide you. For certain housing markets such as Metro Vancouver, we are comfortable with using growth rates close to 7% annually. Below are the historical rates for Vancouver.

Vancouver Home Prices	Start Year	End Year	Annual Rate of Increase
30+ Years	1990	2023	
Average Price	$329,570	$2,490,388	6.3%
20+ Years	2000	2023	
Average Price	$381,502	$2,490,388	8.5%
10+ Years	2010	2023	
Average Price	$807,776	$2,490,388	9%

CMHC Vancouver Housing History

Regarding growth, Vancouver single-family house prices over the last thirty years show well above the 6% annual increase. To be conservative for clients, I would use 6% for the Vancouver/Toronto area for single-family housing, 4% for condos/townhouses. For outside of these areas, I would use between 3-6% for houses, and 1-4% for condos/townhouses depending on the city location.

How do we know these high numbers will continue in the future? Follow the numbers, and let the data guide your decision. Metro Vancouver does not have enough supply to support the demand over the next twenty years. Currently, 1600 units of single and multi-family are built in Vancouver each year. "For Vancouver to close its housing disparity within ten years, it would need a minimum of 2,500 new units per year. This includes 750 affordable housing units for households earning 80% or less of area median income." To understand numerically if housing prices are predicted to be rising or falling we should look at basic supply and demand through the Sales To Active Listing ratio. When the ratio in any area is below 12%, this is a signal that the housing prices are trending down. When the ratio is above 20%, prices are going up. If between 12-20%, as shown in the graph below, then we are in a balanced market. Since 2005, the majority of the time has been aggressively a seller's market. Coupled with the low projected supply to meet projected demand, we can only conclude that our housing prices will mimic the growth of the past, or surpass it.

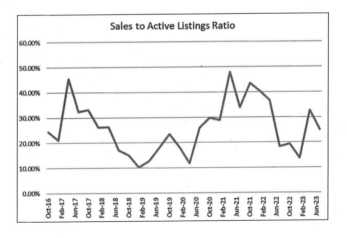

Vancouver's Housing Stock Not Keeping Up With Stock

For Metro Vancouver, this ratio has been significantly above 20% for the majority of the past fifteen years. As can be seen, only during two limited time periods were we in a buyer's market. I have been investing in the Vancouver area for the past twenty years, and I have only known a few short pockets of time when there was not a great demand from buyers. So, if you follow the numbers, not your emotions, you dramatically reduce the risk of making a poor investment.

Fraser Valley Real Estate Monthly Statistics

In comparison, the S&P 500, which is typically the bedrock of most stock portfolios, should be analyzed not only for its returns but also for its volatility. The S&P 500 has returned approximately 9% on average. However, the volatility to get this return is what causes many people to not realize this return. The reason is due to the emotions involved when you are down 35% (2008), or up 21.74% (2021). With stocks, it is very easy to liquidate when you are uneasy, and to buy more when you are overconfident. This will result in selling low and buying high, which erodes many of your gains. With real estate being a very non-liquid asset, you are almost forced to hold it for the long term. Further, the high cost and hassle to sell a property causes investors to really analyze whether or not selling is the best idea. What typically happens is they tend to hold onto their investment during the down periods, and many years later are glad they did not sell.

S&P 500 Stock Market Returns

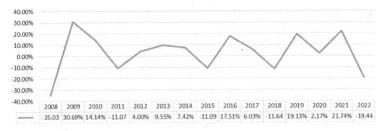

S&P 500 Historical Annual Returns

	2008	2009	2010	2011	2012	2013	2014	2015	2016	2017	2018	2019	2020	2021	2022
	-35.03	30.69%	14.14%	-11.07	4.00%	9.55%	7.42%	-11.09	17.51%	6.03%	-11.64	19.13%	2.17%	21.74%	-19.44

The chart below highlights the volatility of the stock market versus the real estate market (in Metro Vancouver). The stock market returns, year-over-year, are represented by the S&P 500 Returns solid line. The dotted line represents the fluctuations in the real estate market. I have used the Vancouver market, not only because it is my local housing market, but also because due to our high prices, it tends to show the greatest fluctuations. Since 2008, the S&P 500 has had a 17% standard deviation, while the Vancouver real estate market shows only a 6.9% standard deviation. Investors want less volatility in their lives, not more. Their investments are no exception.

Stock vs. Real Estate Volatility
(Annual Percentage Change)

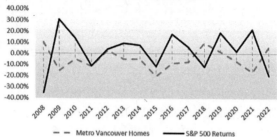

- - Metro Vancouver Homes   ——— S&P 500 Returns

Real Estate Versus Stocks Performance

When comparing two very different investments, we should not only look at the returns. Professional investors will also measure the risk of the asset. William Sharpe created a way to measure the risk versus the reward of any investment. The Sharpe Ratio below is a simple metric to determine the best return when taking the riskiness of the investment into account.

$$\text{Sharpe Ratio Formula} = \frac{(Rp - Rf)}{O'p}$$

The formula simply takes an investment's return, then subtracts out the return of a risk-free alternative investment, such as a GIC. That gives you a "risk premium." You then divide the risk premium over the investment's volatility. This is measured by its annual standard deviation in value. If the math is too confusing, not to worry. All you really need to know is investors will want a high Sharpe Ratio when comparing investments. A Sharpe Ratio, at the time of this writing, for Vanguard S&P 500 Index is .36 (June 9, 2023), while residential real estate is almost double at .7. However, with an individual property, the Sharpe Ratio can be significantly higher than 1 or 2. If you are serious about investing, you should be moving away from friendly advice, and moving towards understanding the math behind your decisions. Individual real estate investors who have made millions more than stock investors did not do it by accident. They better understood the math.

The Advantage of Real Estate Investors Over Stock Investors

What happens to your investments in your retirement? This is where real estate dramatically differs from the stock investment. If you retire with a stock investment portfolio, a traditional financial advisor will need to start changing the mixture of the allocation in order to lower the stock exposure because of its volatility. It is very common when you're in your twenties and thirties to have a 70% stock and 30% bond portfolio, or something similar. The target returns are typically between 6-9%. When you are in your sixties and seventies, the stock portion needs to adjust down to preserve the capital. If the stocks that were driving the higher rates of return are now a lower portion of the portfolio, you can expect a much lower return. Your portfolio might now look like a 30% stock and 70% bond mix. These conservative returns will now yield closer to 3-5%. So the first problem with RRSPs in retirement is the low rates of return. Conversely, the real estate investment will not have this problem. Its rate of growth will remain constant, even into your retirement. Further, you will have two options to take equity out of the real estate when you start to need the money. You can choose to sell, or you can choose to leverage against it.

The second problem with your RRSPs in retirement is that you can outlive your stock investments. They could deplete down to zero. If you have dividend-paying stocks, will the dividends be high enough for you to not deplete the capital in retirement? For the average Canadian, most probably not. Conversely, with several properties in real estate, you can live off the cash-flowing rent without depleting the properties' equity value. Therefore, aside from the superior growth in asset value, as an added bonus we also take into account the rent. Rental rates in Canada increase somewhere between 1-5% annually depending on the city you live in. Over the thirty years of the mortgage, at some point this rent will be enough to pay off all of the property's expenses, such as mortgage, property taxes, HOA fees, maintenance, property management, etc. Once this occurs all of that extra cash is now going towards you personally.

If you can get a good property based on your down payment, then in Year 1, this rent minus the expenses should be cash flowing or at least breakeven. Below is the sample for a $360,000 property. You make a 20% down payment ($72,000), resulting in a $288K mortgage (at 4.5% loan rate over thirty year amortization). As the years go by, notice how the net cash flow you will earn grows. I have assumed that in Year 1, you are breakeven for cash flow. Your DIP advisor has helped you to find a great property in a growing area. We assume annually the property increases at 5%, and inflation causes the rental rate and expenses to both increase by 3%. Expenses will include taxes, HOA fees, maintenance, property management, and all other costs associated with real estate. The table shows what the property value and your cash flow will be in retirement.

	Growth Rates	Age 30	Age 55	Age 65
Property Value	5%	$360,000	$1,219,088	$1,985,765
Mortgage Balance		$288,000	$78,276	$0
Rental Income	3%	$1,900/m	$3,978/m	$5,346/m
Mortgage	4.5%	$1,159/m	$1,459/m	$0
Expenses	3%	$441/m	$923/m	$1,241/m
Net Cash Flow Monthly		$0/m	$1,596/m	$4,105:m
Annual Payout		$0	$19,152	$49,260

To compare against a good dividend-paying Canadian stock, I will use a stock growing at 7%, with dividend yields of 4%/a. If I take the same $72,000 that was used for the real estate down payment, and instead put it in the stock market, then the table below shows both the future value and dividend payout.

	Growth Rates	Age 30	Age 55	Age 65
Value of Stock	7%	$72,000	$390,775	$768,713
Dividend payout annually	4%	$2,880	$15,631	$30,746

Comparing the property to the dividend paying stock at retirement age, we see the real estate outperforms both the asset value and the annual cash flow. If anyone questions using a $360K property in Canada that generates $1900/m in rent, I respond that these criteria were found in multiple locations at the time of this writing in 2023. In fact, the numbers look even better if I used the Airbnb property options at this price point. However, my analysis does have certain scenarios of dividend-paying stocks outperforming real estate but they involve 10.2% rates of annual return with a 7% dividend. However, the average person will not likely be able to find such an investment with those consistent returns over thirty years. As well, if the real estate investor in retirement is able to live solely on the annual cash flow, then at death he can pass on this cash-flowing asset to his children or grandchildren. When the owner turns eighty-five, this one property would be valued at $5,268,827 with an annual cash flow of $88,980. This is the type of exciting legacy I wish all my clients to leave to their kids and grandkids.

Questions to ask yourself: By retirement, if the properties are fully paid, could you live off the rental income? Probably yes. Will you ever outlive the asset? Probably no. How about inflation? This is bad for retirees with traditional investments since their purchasing power is eroded, and their conservative retirement portfolios will make it hard to keep up. Alternatively, inflation is good for real estate properties. Rent goes up with inflation. Further, over time rent tends to exceed the inflation rate especially in popular areas such as Metro Vancouver and the GTA. Stock investments will be struggling to keep up with inflation as they were when inflation peaked at 8.1% in June 2022. During this same year, the S&P 500 was down 22.9% from its peak in 2021, ending the year 18.3% down from its peak. Meanwhile, the Metro Vancouver rental market increased 10.5% in 2022.1 If the average investor decides to adopt this philosophy of real estate as a retirement vehicle, and invests in only two to three properties, their wealth ceiling will surely be broken.

Median Rents for Two-bedroom Apartment in Vancouver 2009 to 2022

Appendix 6

What is Wrong with DIY Investing?

"Your ego is not your amigo." Mark Walberg

What about DIY investing? You may have seen numbers on how much you will save by doing it yourself, saving on 1-2% fees going to an investment advisor in the form of high MERs. Over a lifetime of investing, your returns diminish when the advisor is simply investing in a balanced portfolio that was correlated to the S&P 500 index or something similar.

You may have also heard that the average financial investment advisor (FIA) does not even beat the S&P 500. So, why on earth would you have someone else manage your money? Why not manage it yourself? An article written by Eric Rosenberg, Investorjunkie.com, compares two portfolios, one investing in low-fee index funds, and the other using an Actively Managed Fund. If both yielded the same rate of return, the erosion at retirement would be the result of high management fees. He uses an initial investment of $5000, with a $250/m contribution for thirty years. He assumes an 8% average annualized rate of return. He then compares using a Robo Advisor that rebalances a portfolio automatically and charges .25% in annual fees to a traditional FIA that charges 1-2% in fees.

	Initial Investment	Monthy Investment	MER Fees	30-year total Net Worth	Extra Amount loss to FIA fees	Age 65
DIY	$5,000	$250/m	.25%	$317,433	0%	0%
Advisor 1%	$5,000	$250/m	1%	$273,274	$44,159	-13.9%
Advisor 2%	$5,000	$250/m	2%	$224,529	$92,904	-29.3%

As you can see, you are losing almost 30% of your net worth to fees, unless your advisor can consistently beat the basic index fund market.

Robo Advisors Versus Financial Advisors

What do many DIY investors do? The most common practice is dollar cost averaging using index funds. Three main goals are achieved with this method. First, you are diversifying by buying the top 500 stocks in the US market. You don't have to worry about picking the winners; the S&P 500 will pick them for you. Second, you don't have to worry about trying to time the market. You are simply putting aside a set amount of money each month, investing in the same index repeatedly. At the time of this writing, the S&P 500 had a ten-year average return of 8% annualized. And third, by buying each month you are not timing the market to figure out whether you're buying at a high or a low. Over time this strategy has yielded a solid 8-10% return, not adjusted for inflation. Fourth, you are saving on MER fees.

There are now many low-fee platforms, such as Vanguard or Questrade that allow you to dollar cost average with the

S&P 500. You save on fees. And since most of the advisors cannot beat the market, why would you pay someone an added fee?

However, there are several problems with DIY investing. First, most investors do not have the discipline to stick to the strategy. They may start with dollar cost averaging. But when markets are really getting hammered, such as in 2008 or 2020, they are tempted to start investing less or, perhaps, more. This goes against dollar cost averaging since that is now attempting to time the market. Second, as you start to learn more about investing, greater knowledge can also be a curse. You might start reading blogs, or getting into group chats with friends and colleagues about what they are doing with investing. When you learn that they are making a fortune in Bitcoin, Tesla, marijuana stocks, or even shorting stocks, you might feel fear of missing out and start veering from your strategy.

Be honest with yourself: Are you a DIY investor with the intention of dollar cost averaging? And if so, have you veered away in any form, such as what I have described? If yes, then you are going against the dollar cost averaging strategy.

Some people might take a portion of their portfolio such as 30% to buy individual stocks then they simply dollar cost average with the remaining amount. However, with these stocks they will be trying to time the market. If you are a DIY investor, remember: you need to calculate your entire portfolio, the good years, as well as the bad years. Most people will not take the time to do this. They start to consider the stocks that have flopped as if they were gambling money. At the time of this writing in 2023, Tesla is now down 35%, Bitcoin is down 40% and the S&P 500 down 15%. If you exposed yourself to any of these investments, are you calculating your total returns?

The final problem with dollar cost averaging is a very

simple one. You will not become rich. I'm talking about my definition of rich, which is generational wealth without giving up an abundant lifestyle. If you need a number, I will give you the number $5M, not including your home. I believe $5M is enough money to support a comfortable retirement in Canada as well as setting up two generations with a starting point for their financial lives.

To achieve this number, from age twenty-five to age sixty-five, you would have had to contribute over $2,000 per month into a dollar cost averaging strategy in the S&P 500 returning a 7% ROI in order to achieve the $5M. For the average Canadian, that is not reasonable. How can you still achieve this? The DIP strategy I am urging in this book seeks that same $5M target with neither the volatility of the stock market nor the monthly investment needed from dollar cost averaging.

As a DIY stock picker or a day trader, you have the difficult task of trying to pick the winners and the losers. Will there be winners? And will there actually be losers in stocks? Absolutely. Look at the many stocks that have an intrinsic value of almost zero that were worth billions of dollars just a decade ago. But for real estate the formula is simpler because the game is simpler. You just need to pick a future long-term winner and for real estate the majority of all real estate will fall into this category. There is no Canadian real estate that is worth less today than it was twenty years ago and there is also almost no Canadian real estate that does not support an average rental market return. Your larger challenge will be ensuring that it is not a headache over the years you own the property.

For the DIYer who is willing to spend even more time researching stocks, you have to realize what you are doing is actually taking on another job. There is opportunity cost money lost when you spend all of your extra time on blogs and reading articles on the sectors and individual stocks. What you are trying to do is to get better information to have an edge on getting better than average index returns. Even if you did this in your past with such moves as Bitcoin, Game Stop, or Tesla, can you be consistent in getting the same return over thirty or forty years of investing? It is similar to being a gambler who researches how to get an edge on the game. It can be time consuming, and not achieve the end result you were hoping for. Investing is no different. It's laudable to be interested enough in your finances to learn to invest on your own. However, don't let your stepping stone become your gravestone. If you are not getting the results you want, get someone else involved. If you believe you can do better with real estate, get a DIP advisor involved.

For the real estate investor, the formula is simple: 99% of real estate investments will be winners in the future, as long as you find something that is cash flowing or breakeven. If you are going to DIY in the stock market, you will be using up a lot of your time in life in the hopes of doing better than the stock market average returns by saving on fees. I believe you will save on fees, but will not get rich. As well, if you were good at finding a winning stock, how much will you possibly invest in this winner? Maybe $5,000? Maybe $20,000? For real estate investors, when we find a winning property, we will put $100K+ to invest. For example, if we found a $1M cash-flowing property that is being sold at $900,000, we will put $180,000 down payment on this undervalued property in a heartbeat. We will one day own the entire $1M asset, which will continue to cash flow. This is much better use of our time to research and find a winning investment. Think carefully about your objective for DIY. I believe getting rich with help is better than staying mediocre on your own.

How to contact us

We work primarily with individuals and companies across Canada based on a fee-for-service model. If you are interested in learning more about working with us, we look forward to connecting with you.

Website: www.latitude-west.ca
Email: cdy@latitude-west.ca

Our Website

My Financial Practice

When I took over my father's financial practice, I not only gained forty years of experience but also brought my desire for helping clients to invest in real estate. I realized that traditional financial advisors were only focusing on wealth in the stock market, which limited them from growing assets exponentially. My practice is now focused on working with clients who want to build their financial wealth in both the real estate and the stock markets. This is achieved with an integration of stock assets combined with active and passive real estate investments. My team does traditional financial planning for clients, but also analyzes and presents new cash-flowing real estate deals for them to invest in.

Latitude West Financial is partnered with investment-focused real estate teams across Canada, the US, and Mexico. With this unique service offering, we are able to analyze and present outstanding investment deals to our clients. We offer fee-for-service advice, which allows for transparency and nonbiased recommendations. Our goal is to ensure that when the markets go up and down, our investment clients do not. This occurs by investing in non-correlated assets, which seeks to preserve capital while growing exponentially. We want to be safe in all seasons of a market cycle, and to be positioned to take advantage of opportunities in any season.

Personally, I have a passion for giving financial workshops and educating younger families just starting out. I enjoy travelling to look at properties, and creating financial content to educate more people on how to create wealth. In my spare time, I enjoy time with my family, as well as volunteering with my church, and leading teams abroad with my projects overseas in Asia and Central America.

Acknowledgements

I would like to thank my wife Karen and three daughters, Olivia, Madeline, and Isabella, for their support and encouragement for me to write this book. Our journey together continues to be nothing short of amazing. As well, special gratitude goes towards my Uncle Cesar, for teaching me to invest, and my Auntie Em, for showing me how to help others in need. Finally, a special thanks to my parents, Leo and Christie, and my in-laws, Allan and Caroline. They sacrificed by leaving their loved ones and immigrating to this country, hoping for a better life for them and their kids. I thank them for their unconditional loving support for our family. We are eternally grateful.